DATE			
REFERENCE			

FORM 125 M

Ride & Tie

Ride & Tie

The Challenge of Running and Riding
by Donald T. Jacobs

REF
GV
1063.5
.J32

cop. 1

© 1978 by
World Publications
Box 366, Mountain View, CA 94042

No information in this book may be reprinted in
any form without permission from the publisher.

Library of Congress Number 78-365
ISBN 0-89037-099-0

To my daughter, Jessica London;
may you always strive toward your potential
as you play the game of life.

Table of Contents

Foreword

The Ride & Tie is a unique race, ostensibly derived from old Wild West days, when two men sometimes had to cover long miles with only one horse between them. Since the inception of the modern race in 1970, its popularity among cowboy types and marathoners—both tough breeds—has grown yearly.

Partly to determine the reasons for this popularity, and partly because of the unusual challenge, I, too, was lured to the Ride & Tie in 1977. As an experienced marathoner teamed up with an expert runner/rider, I figured a fifteen- to twenty-mile run interspersed with restful intervals on horseback would be a piece of cake. I was dead wrong.

I had forgotten the key element that makes Ride & Tie the most unpredictable, exasperating, and intriguing footrace in America—our four-legged partner, the horse. Our little Arabian mare, not as experienced as her human teammates, was delayed by the vets. I ended up running twenty-seven hilly miles instead of the planned twenty, and staggered to the finish bruised, scratched, exhausted, and stiff, with the beginnings of a horrendous case of poison oak. My partner and our perverse Arabian had finished several minutes earlier, and we salvaged fifteenth place, out of the money. It was the toughest race of my life, but I immediately determined that I'd try again next year. So did all the other contestants who rode or staggered in for hours after us.

What kind of race can be simultaneously the most grueling and exciting in this country? Don Jacobs, an accomplished rider, runner, and successful Ride & Tie veteran, explores this question in depth in his book about this unique event. In anecdote and narrative, he captures the flavor and variety of the annual Ride & Tie, and offers tested training advice for both biped and quadruped competitors. Past, present, and would-be participants will enjoy this account of the race with the silent, but essential, third partner.

Joan Ullyot, M.D.

Introduction

*Picture, if you will, 200 humans and
100 horses hoofing it across more than
30 miles of narrow, dusty trails, steep
uphill climbs, scorching, grassy plains,
suicidal slopes and rocky, calamitous
canyons. Add blisters, bruised and aching
joints, scraped shins, fatigue, thirst,
adrenaline gone berserk, determination and
Gatorade. Mix them together and you've got
yourself . . . a Ride & Tie. A helluva way to go!**

My first introduction to Ride & Tie was at a prerace barbeque in 1976. The affair was held in a camper-strewn field
surrounded by the Sierra Nevada mountain range. The rugged
scent of horses and leather permeated the fresh mountain air.
Steaks and chicken sizzled on open grills and music blared
from a variety of portable radios. As the summer sun seemed
to touch the distant mountain peaks, the air began to cool
and half-naked bodies donned jackets and sweatshirts.

Aside from the leaner than average physiques and a myriad
of multicolored running shoes, the group was relatively in-
conspicuous. One lady, with freckles and long, red hair, was
dancing with her teenage son. A young man, hardly older
than ten, was pinning a number on his running shorts as he
clutched a savory chicken leg between his teeth. A grey-
haired gentleman was proudly displaying a horse for his
grandchildren. One would not have guessed that in two days
they would be participating in one of the most challenging
distance races in the world.

*Helga Charnes, "Over the Bounding Mane," *WomenSports*, October
1975, p. 59.

In observing the group, it was difficult to determine who were the runners and who were just members of a team's pit crew. Nor did eavesdropping offer any clues. At one table, a professor of zoology from North Carolina was conversing about human physiology. A physician was discussing horse-breeding at another table. At a third, a San Francisco fire fighter and a Seattle stockbroker were planning an abalone dive. One group was discussing watering techniques for house plants.

Not until race time did I see what uniqueness of character had been resting quietly behind the group's common image. Only when they were lined up at the start of the race did I perceive an array of bold knights and foot soldiers, courageously prepared to join in an intimate struggle with the elements of nature. The rugged terrain, the unpredictable circumstances, heat, fatigue, and time would be met head-on with a spirit of competition that joined together, rather than separated, opposing teams.

Then it happened. The race began and I found myself moving, almost involuntarily, amidst a thundering roar of war whoops and galloping hooves. I decided, at the last minute, to participate in the race in place of a runner who dropped out. Now, here I was, feeling like a dismounted roughrider charging up San Juan Hill. I had never been more excited.

All I knew at the time was that I was to keep my eyes open for my teammate's horse, which was to be tied somewhere ahead of me on the course. When I reached the horse, I was to mount and continue riding until I caught up with my teammate, who would have been running from the time he tied the horse. I would then ride past him a self-determined distance, tie the horse to a tree or post, and continue on foot once again. When my partner reached the horse, he would mount and ride past me, thus repeating the cycle.

The idea was to keep leap-frogging past each other in this fashion, with the horse resting in between, until our entire eight-legged team managed to cross the finish line some thirty miles away. We would be required to tie the horse a minimum of six times along the trail and report the tying to one of the many field referees located at various points along the trail. And finally, we would have to be sure that our horse re-

mained in good enough condition to pass the mandatory veterinarian checks en route. It sounded simple enough. After
all, if the twelve-year-old boy and the seventy-year-old man
could do it, it couldn't be too difficult.

I couldn't have been more mistaken. At the outset, I nar-
rowly escaped being trampled by the stampede of excited
horses as they exploded across the starting line. Clouds of
dust veiled the rock-strewn trail and twice I stumbled, barely
managing to regain my momentum before being overtaken by
a galloping horse or runner. By the time I reached the top of
the first hill, less than a mile from the start, my body looked
and felt as though it had climbed up one side of a mountain
and rolled down the other.

To compound the difficulties, I almost overran my awaiting horse at the first tie. As a result, I was compelled to keep
one eye on the difficult trail and one in constant search for
the horse. The occasional appearance of a riderless horse
storming down a hill added the worry that I might never
reach my horse at all. Fortunately, the prospect of having to
run the entire course on foot was always dispelled by the
awaiting animal.

However, just as the relief of having reached my horse began to illuminate my countenance, the apprehension of having to ride him down the side of the rocky mountain began
to curl my lips. I had already observed one woman participant and her horse roll head over heels down an embankment. Although they were uninjured and managed to continue the race in good form, the excitability of my horse
made a repeat performance seem very probable. The act of
untying him, keeping him out of the way of oncoming teams,
and trying to mount him on the uneven terrain made the
thought of running the whole race less dreadful.

But there was never time for such thoughts to linger very
long. Somewhere out there was my partner, running his heart
out and waiting for me to pass him on horseback. My responsibility to provide him with a sound horse to ride before he
had run too great a distance left no time for self-pity. The
rugged beauty of the landscape was starting to stir more enjoyable emotions. The friendly competition, struggling
against the same elements as I, brought comfort to my mis-

Following an exciting start, the field begins to space out at the first hill in the 1976 Tahoe Ride & Tie. (Scotty Ray Morris)

ery. And, in just a few, full-packed hours, I would be a proud member of the Ride & Tie family, sharing memories that would last, at least until the next race.

There was no doubt that I would participate in the next Ride & Tie. Even as I forced my bruised and depleted body to dance during the evening celebration, I was secretly planning a training program and game strategy. Next year I would at least be able to dance as energetically as those on the team that had crossed the finish line twenty minutes ahead of us.

I am now preparing for a third Ride & Tie event—just as I will be preparing for a fourth, fifth, sixth, and so on. In the meantime, I feel compelled to share the Ride & Tie story. This book is a comprehensive guide to the sport of Ride & Tie. It covers every aspect of the sport from conditioning and training a team to planning a strategy and organizing your own Ride & Tie event. The information on physical fitness, nutrition, running, and horsemanship will enable you to successfully complete your first Ride & Tie, regardless of your present level of fitness or your ability as a runner or an equestrian.

Throughout its pages, this book also attempts to describe what it is like to participate in the wildest, toughest, and most fascinating game around—a game for the running enthusiast, the equestrian, and the adventurer. You will see how

Ride & Tie can capsulize the drama of a lifetime into a single experience. You will understand how this experience of learning, excitement, challenge, reward, and frustration has actually changed people's lives. And most importantly, you will learn that Ride & Tie can be an enjoyable objective with which to achieve the goal of optimal physical and mental health and well-being.

Part One
First Steps to Ride & Tie

1
The Challenge

Take hold the test
To try your best
And see what you can do.
Take careful aim
When you play the game
And the meaning of life will come through.

Before you accept the Ride & Tie challenge it is essential that you fully comprehend the task ahead. Without this realization you will lose the opportunity to express your full potential, and you will not be able to test yourself validly. What would otherwise be a rewarding experience could become a frustrating ordeal. It would be foolish to prepare for this game without knowing the magnitude of its challenge. Foolhardiness, says Dr. George Sheehan, will not help us find the edge between our possibilities and self-destruction. He says further that "to arrive at that place, you have to have preparation in strength and speed and endurance. You have to know what to do and when to do it."*

The challenge of Ride & Tie has become its most notable trademark. Chuck Stalley, one of the outstanding competitors in the Levi's National Ride & Tie since the first race in 1971, tells a story that confirms this reputation. Chuck was being interviewed for a job as a high school teacher. The principal who was conducting the interview asked Chuck if there was anything else he would like to add to his qualifications or past experience. Chuck thought for a moment and said, "No, that about covers it. The only other thing is that I have participated in the Levi's Ride & Tie race since 1971 and have taken first place twice." The principal gleamed. He was familiar with the race. Closing the file on his desk, he told

*George Sheehan, *Dr. Sheehan on Running* (Mountain View, Calif.: World Publications, 1975), p. 72.

1

Chuck that the job was his. "If you can do that, you can do anything," the principal remarked.

Others attest to the mighty challenge of Ride & Tie. John Barnes, a former Olympian, twice National Collegiate Athletic Association (NCAA) half-mile champion, and a member of a world-record relay team, said completing Ride & Tie in forty-third place was "equal to and in some respects more demanding than my past accomplishments."* Joe Amlong, a Ride and Tie competitor and Olympic gold medalist in the 1964 Tokyo rowing competition, calls Ride & Tie "a race for masochists." Although an unfair appraisal, his comment is expressive of the grueling challenge facing the serious competitor. Ken Williams, a nationally ranked half-miler in high school, describes the challenge with more reverence. He sees Ride & Tie as the ultimate way to express himself as a runner, and describes the "tremendous mental appeal" as being similar to chess. Moves can be calculated against just enough variables to experience "the perfect game." And yet, despite the fact that he has won the Levi's National Ride & Tie twice, Williams continues to dub Ride & Tie "the toughest game."

Not everyone who competes in Ride & Tie is so enthusiastic about its challenge. Some, like Gordon Ainsleigh and Rick Sylvester, seem nonchalant about such challenges. But then Ainsleigh was the first man to run the grueling 100-mile Tevis Cup horse race entirely on foot in less than twenty-four hours. And Rick Sylvester was the first man to ski off El Capitan in Yosemite National Park. (Sylvester had more luck with that daring event than in three years of attempting to finish the Ride & Tie.)

Respect the Challenge

If you are aspiring to compete in Ride & Tie you should respect its challenge. With this respect, you will be better equipped to appraise the various components of the challenge and be able to prepare more realistically. Training for Ride & Tie should be an enjoyable effort, but it should also be a thorough one.

*Bud Johns, "A Race for Masochists?" *True Magazine,* December 1975, p. 52.

People often ask, "What is the most difficult aspect of the Ride & Tie?" The answer varies from one contestant to another. For an experienced endurance rider, running may be the most difficult. Most equestrians have never considered sharing the task of transportation with the horse—at least not at the ground level. For these individuals the sight of the horse tied to a tree during the race is a bit of heaven. Even tired, bone-weary riders seem to have little problem getting back in the saddle after an exhausting run. But can you imagine their dread at having to get off again and continue on foot?

One equestrienne competing in a Ride & Tie was observed riding her horse to a tie spot. She dismounted, patted her horse sorrowfully on the neck, and began a slow, limping jog around a bend in the trail. Within a minute she reappeared, untied her horse, and remounted. A peek around the corner revealed a steep hill that she apparently felt could be better handled by her teammate. She then tied at the top of the hill.

On the other hand, there are those veteran distance runners who are not comfortable with horses. For them riding is the most difficult component. They become dejected when they must consider stopping their run to mount a nervous, excited, one-thousand-pound horse, as eager to continue running as they are.

One runner in the Northstar Tahoe (California) Ride & Tie paced himself comfortably until he arrived at his horse. Then he slowed down, gritted his teeth, and carefully untied the lead line. The trail where the horse had been tied was narrow and ran alongside a steep embankment. As the man attempted to get his foot in the stirrup, the horse sidestepped, pushing him over the ledge. Fortunately, the man held on to the lead line and managed to climb back up the hill. By now the horse had become quite impatient with the fellow, and began tossing his head and turning in circles. After considerable effort, the man set off on foot once again, with the horse running riderless alongside him.

Still others claim the most difficult part of Ride & Tie is the prerace logistics. Indeed, it is sometimes a challenge just finding teammates for the race. Although considerations for borrowing or buying a horse will be dealt with in a later chapter, you should not overlook the importance of selecting an appropriate human partner. In spite of the difficulty of finding a suitable human partner, there is usually someone willing to seriously consider the venture. It just requires a bit of salesmanship to bring out the dormant adventurer in someone. Even after someone has agreed, however, you should be prepared for "buyer's remorse." The attrition rate for prospective Ride & Tie partners is high. Unless you know the person well, it is best not to depend totally on his commitment.

One way to handle this problem, if you suspect such a possibility, is to have a back-up teammate. This individual can help train and condition the horse while learning to ride and run well himself. To avoid hurt feelings, there should be a clear understanding that this person is the alternate. If your original partner remains dedicated and injury-free, the alternate will make an excellent pit crew member. Furthermore, if he chooses, the alternate may have a good opportunity to compete in the race with another team. This is because most teams don't plan on having alternates, and very often someone is unable to show for the race. Some individuals even travel hundreds of miles to a Ride & Tie without a horse or a partner lined up, in hopes of joining an incomplete team before the race. This, in fact, is how I entered my first Ride & Tie in 1976. The day before the race I spread the word that I would be available if anyone with a horse needed a partner. Late in the afternoon a man of Japanese ancestry approached me. "You want to run?" he asked. Alongside him was a lean Arabian mare that looked like she could do the job. I shook his hand and said, "You bet." At that he handed me a long braided lead rope attached to a 3/8-inch rope halter. "You ride," he directed.

I naturally assumed he wanted to be sure I could ride his horse. If I could stay on bareback and without a bridle, perhaps I would do all right in the saddle. But I began to worry when this gentleman's good friend and "translator" explained to me that my new partner, Masiji Terasawa from Reseda, California, was accustomed to riding fifty-mile races without a saddle or bridle. I was able to convince "Max" (as I came to call him) that I was willing to ride without a bridle, but that a saddle was a must.

The next day Max appeared at the starting line in combat boots and long, baggy pants. But whatever he lacked in his image as a runner, he made up for with his style as a rider. At one point in the race I had been running a considerable distance and the horse had not yet passed me. All of a sudden I heard Max yelling, "Number four, number four" (our team number). He approached me at a fast, extended trot, and without causing the horse to miss a stride, he swung off the horse and handed me the lead rope. The horse continued past me until the slack in the rope was gone, and I was forced to follow. Running as fast as I could, I hopped up and pulled myself onto the saddle, as I struggled to fit my boots in the stirrups. To Max, this maneuver must have been standard procedure.

Max and I placed twenty-third in the race. He proved to be as tough and considerate an individual as he was skilled as a rider. Although we have not met since, our friendship has been bonded forever.

Signing up for a Ride & Tie race without a predetermined team, thus, may be worthwhile. Alternates should realize that they have a good opportunity to compete in the Ride & Tie even if both original partners remain as a team. With this in mind, alternates can dedicate themselves to the challenge as seriously and energetically as other competitors. Then, if they are needed, they will be ready.

Partner Compatibility

One consideration in choosing and training with another person relates to compatibility. The issues that arise in preparation for a Ride & Tie race are similar to those faced in making a trans-Atlantic crossing in a small boat. The shared responsibilities, the frustrations of horse problems and personal progress, the conflicting opinions on training and strategy, plus the many hours spent together in preparation can be threatening, even to the best of friendships. But awareness of this difficulty is usually enough to avoid it.

Since many people ignore the mental challenge of Ride & Tie, this aspect is often overlooked in training. Although most of these considerations will be discussed in the chapter on strategy and tactics, it is important to realize at the outset of training that concentration is paramount in Ride & Tie.

For example, many runners have accidentally run past their horses in Ride & Tie competition. Depending on how many miles you have covered before you realize the mistake, the resulting run back can be painfully depressing as well as embarrassing.

I was fortunate enough to learn this lesson the easy way. My partner and I were off to a good start in the 1977 Levi's Ride & Tie. I began the race riding, and tied up my horse after about two miles. When my partner passed me on horseback, I was on a gentle down-sloping hill and running strong. When they passed me I started running even faster, determined to maintain our good position. The adrenalin of the start was still flowing through my veins when I realized that my shoelace had come untied. I hated the thought of stopping, but the shoe was beginning to loosen on my foot. I stopped at the side of the road and hastily began pulling at my shoelace. As I was completing the tie, I looked back up the road to make sure no horse traffic was coming. There, before my eyes, and five yards up the road, was my horse. From that point on I was a large pair of eyes drifting over a small pair of feet.

Other competitors have had to learn the hard way. Larry Mannix of Tucson overran his horse in a local, twenty-four-mile Ride & Tie race near Phoenix, Arizona. Since long runs were a part of his team's strategy, he was not alarmed after covering about four miles. However, after about five miles he began getting angry at his partner for riding so far. By this time Larry's partner was worried that something had happened to the horse or to Larry. So Larry's partner turned around and slowly started back. At about the same time, assuming that he had passed the horse, Larry also turned around. Both teammates questioned passing riders, but none were able to give any helpful answers. After about four miles of backtracking, Larry's partner became convinced that something had gone wrong, and increased his pace. However, Larry, who was crying, cursing, and praying at the same time, was still unsure. Maybe he should have continued a few more yards before turning around. In a few more miles he would have to turn around again and head for the finish. But just when things seemed hopeless, Larry saw the horse tied to the base of a cactus stalk. Larry's team eventually finished the race second to last, having run an extra ten miles. (I don't know what happened to the last-place team.)

This race was Larry's first Ride & Tie competition. But many experienced competitors have made the same mistake. Jim Remillard from Chico, California, overran his horse by three miles in the 1975 Levi's Ride & Tie. Jim has won the Brown's Ride & Tie twice and competed in the National Ride & Tie six times, five times placing in the top ten.

Another veteran competitor, ex-Olympian John Emery from San Francisco, ran past his horse in the 1974 Tahoe race. In the 1977 Levi's Ride & Tie, John and his partner, Bill Kirschmeir of Larkspur, California, rode an all-white horse to an excellent tenth-place finish. Bill claims the white horse was used so that John "couldn't miss it."

Mental lapses can get teams other than your own in trouble. One year, in the National Ride & Tie, Rick Sylvester and his teammate were unable to finish the race because someone had accidentally untied their horse and it ran away. The culprit, thinking the horse was his own, was not ready for the response of the strange animal, and dropped the tie rope. The horse ran to the finish riderless, and Rick and his partner finished the race on foot.

In the 1976 Levi's Ride & Tie, twelve-year-old Donnie Browning almost made a similar mistake. In response to an interview he explained, "I don't ever pass my horse because I'm too tired. But once I hit the wrong horse for putting his ears back." Fortunately, he was saved from further consequences when he heard a gruff voice exclaim, "Hey young man, what are you doing to my horse?"

This need for continual mental concentration is often most frustrating to the experienced long-distance runner. Dr. Joan Ullyot, after participating in her first Ride & Tie, described the problem: "When you are running a marathon, it is possible to let your thoughts drift somewhat. However, in Ride & Tie you must constantly be aware of what is going on around you." If you must be constantly aware of what is going on around you, it is difficult to maintain the inner awareness that helps push the marathon runner past various psychological barriers. Often in Ride & Tie, just when a runner has found a groove, he must readapt to a new situation. This constant readaption often causes physical and psychological difficulties for a trained long-distance runner, who has not trained specifically for Ride & Tie. The experienced runner is normally accustomed to relaxing the leg muscles after a long run by a gradual slow-down and a session of stretching exercises. This prevents the runner from getting leg cramps by gradually removing the accumulation of lactic acid. It also prevents the runner from accidentally pulling tightened running muscles. During a Ride & Tie, the runner must suddenly stop his run. Then, the individual must maintain a horseback-riding position in which leg muscles are in a static, contracted position. By the time he is ready to tie the horse and continue on foot, he may have difficulty walking, let alone running.

The distance runner may also be unaccustomed to the terrain of Ride & Tie courses. Even versatile pentathletes may be taken aback by Ride & Tie courses. The modern pentathlon is the only international event that includes cross-country competition. However, as the many pentathletes who have entered Ride & Ties will attest, there is a big difference between 4,000 meters and forty miles of cross-country terrain. One's first glimpse of a typical Ride & Tie course can be a shock. "It had never occurred to me that man or beast would be called on to race over such terrain," said Duke zoology professor Peter Klopfer after competing in the Paso Robles Ride & Tie. "The race was more difficult than any marathon I have ever run or ever expect to run." On a preride of the same race, one woman cried in disbelief. The woman, Joyce Taylor, had called the sponsors of the race from her home in Arkansas months earlier to inquire about the terrain for training purposes. The reply was "gently, rolling hills." After the race she sobbed, "In Arkansas these are called mountains." Halfway through the preride of the Marin County (California) Ride & Tie, first-time Ride & Tier Jim Prince exclaimed, "Oh my God, this can't be." And he hadn't yet seen the second half of the course.

Thus Ride & Tie offers a special running challenge to even the most talented runners. It is a race that can equalize a world-class runner with a beginning runner. For example,

A Ride & Tie race course usually includes an abundance of challenging hills, turns, and thick brush. (Scotty Ray Morris)

Brad Varner, twenty-six, and Dick Seamans, thirty-two, of Sequim, Washington, had not been runners before entering the 1977 Levi's Ride & Tie. And yet Brad, Dick, and their roping quarter horse Joe finished the race fourteenth, ahead of many sub-three-hour marathon runners and world-class athletes riding endurance-tested Arabians.

Training and Dedication

In the same race, my own experience also demonstrated that Ride & Tie requires more training and dedication than mere distance running. Not only was I considered a beginning runner, with only a year of distance running experience, but my partner, Norm Kreuter, was a 200-pound former football player—not exactly an ideal distance runner or jockey. Even our horse, an eleven-year-old, backyard-bred Arabian, had never been tested in an endurance race. However, by knowing the challenge and training systematically, Norm and I managed to finish fifth, in spite of an inhibiting injury Norm received during the race.

This is not to say that being a world-class runner is not an advantage if the individual works at it. Tom Laris, who has run a 2:16 marathon, has placed second in a Boston Marathon, and has received medals in the Pan American and

Olympic Games, is a good example. It took Tom four years of Ride & Tie attempts to finish in the lead, when in 1977 he finished first with his teammate Ken Williams and his horse Gray.

By now you may be gaining some respect for the challenge of Ride & Tie. Although it does not entail the risk of sports like skydiving, motorcycle racing, or mountain climbing, it does involve testing your ability to endure. Displays of courage are common in Ride & Tie competition, whether the individual is young or old, man or woman. Dawn Damas, a vivacious schoolteacher from Stinson Beach, California, and six-time women's division champion in Levi's Ride & Tie races, once ran a race with a broken heel. Another time she finished a race with a sprained ankle. "Pain is like any confrontation," she explains. "You face it and one party has to back down." Sharon O'Halloran, thirty-one, a bank escrow officer from Santa Monica, entered a race while still recovering from a broken shoulder, suffered in a fall from her horse during training. She also raced with bandaged fingers, slashed when her horse slipped off a dusty embankment.*

Joyce Spearman, thirty-three, a registered nurse, ran eleven miles in one race with double vision and a 5/8-inch piece of oak stuck in her shin after her horse carried her over an eight-foot ravine. The next year Joyce returned to compete again. Like Joyce, once an individual has faced the challenge of Ride & Tie, he is likely to compete again, regardless of the experience. The attrition rate for Ride & Tie contestants is very low, unlike that for motorcycle racing or skydiving. "You have to be a sucker for punishment to enter this race more than once," a Levi Strauss official once said. "But we get lots and lots of repeats. They get hooked on it."

Is such determination masochistic, as it is often described in newspaper accounts? To the contrary, it is an expression of our need to test ourselves again and again. Only by testing our limits, can we fully express our potential. If it were less challenging, the rewards would diminish proportionately. Ask any ten contestants why they are competing in the race, and they will all say it's the challenge. Each may say it in a different way, but the answer is always the same.

*Helga Charnes, "Over the Bounding Mane," *WomenSports,* October 1975, p. 59.

Dawn Damas, six-time "All-Women Team" winner, concentrates on making it up a steep embankment. (Scotty Ray Morris)

But the challenge, to have meaning, must be met with preparation. When we prepare for a Ride & Tie, we remind ourselves that we are to some extent in control of our destinies. Jerry Bestpitch, a young Coast Guard rescue worker, puts it this way: "If I can do this when I don't really have to, I know I can do it when I must."

2
Development of the Sport

A hitch and a hike
Is all that it took
To traverse the old western trails.
Two men and one horse
Could keep far ahead
Of easterners riding on rails.

The development of Ride & Tie as a sport can be discussed from three different perspectives. The first is the historical application of Ride & Tie as a means of transportation. The second involves its development as a sport. And the third has to do with the Ride & Tie experience as it relates to the evolution of modern man.

A Means of Transportation

In historical perspective, the Ride & Tie concept was born with man's earliest relationship with the horse. Most historians believe that the horse was used as a riding animal before it was used to pull. Hieroglyphics depict riding horses as far back as 1500 B.C. Since this date precedes the earliest records of cavalry, we can speculate that horses were originally used for peaceful transportation.

However plausible this assumption, there is no doubt that horses soon became a major tool of war. Horses gave the early conquerors a great advantage over foot soldiers in battle, and allowed them the mobility to expand their dominion. Alexander the Great once built an entire city to honor his faithful steed. Similarly, the American plains Indians valued the horse above all other things.

The early horse and rider shared a mutual need to endure. The nomadic tribes and the ancient armies rode hundreds of miles across unknown territory. In many instances the men outnumbered the horses, since horses were often killed in battle or even eaten for food. It is likely that when time was of the essence, with armies threatened by pursuing enemies or ominous weather, horses were shared in order to make faster time. In *The Art of Travel; or, Shifts and Contrivances Available in Wild Countries*, published in 1855, reference is made to such a practice. The author, Francis Galton, describes how to make a "hurried retreat": "When a party, partly of horsemen and partly footmen, are running away from danger as hard as they can, the footmen lay hold of the stirrup-leathers of the riders, to assist them."* If the party wanted to continue the retreat for some distance and with less urgency, the method of travel known as Ride & Tie would surely have been used.

The first reference made to this method of travel, however, is found in Henry Fielding's *History of Joseph Andrews*. This reference, published in 1885, is worth quoting in its entirety:

> Mr. Adams discharged the bill, and they were both setting out, having agreed to ride and tie, a method of travelling much used by persons who have but one horse between them, and is thus performed. The two travellers set out together, one on horseback, the other on foot: now, as it outgoes him on foot, the custom is, that, when he arrives at the distance agreed on, he is to dismount, tie the horse to some gate, tree, post, or other thing, and then proceed on foot; when the other comes up to the horse he unties him, mounts, and gallops on, till, having passed by his fellow-traveller, he likewise arrives at the place of tying. And this is that method of travelling so much in use among our prudent ancestors, who knew that horses had mouths as well as legs, and that they could not use the latter without being at the expense of suffering the beasts themselves to use the former. This was the method in use in those days when, instead of a coach and six, a member of parliament's Lady used to mount a pillion behind her husband; and a grave sergeant at law condescended to amble to Westminster on an easy pad, with his clerk kicking his heels behind him.**

*Francis Galton, *The Art of Travel* (Garrisburg, G.B.: Stackpole Books, 1855), p. 317.

**Henry Fielding, *History of Joseph Andrews* (London: White, Stokes, and Allen, 1885), pp. 107-8.

From this it would appear that Ride & Tie transportation had made its transition from a means of survival to a common socioeconomic accommodation. It is even possible that the word *hitchhike* was originally descriptive of such a practice. I make this observation based on the *Oxford English Dictionary*'s definition of the two words, *hitch* and *hike*. A *hitch* is an interference in a horse pace or a temporary stoppage. As a verb it is defined as tying up a horse, as to a hitching post. Similarly, *hike* is defined as an extended march over rough terrain or a laborious undertaking. It would certainly seem plausible that hitching and hiking originally described the mode of transportation across rugged lands whereby a rider would hitch his horse and continue hiking, leaving the animal for his travelling companion to use. Historian Ann McGovern describes "ride-and-tie" as a common way to travel in colonial America.* This is a further indication that the word *hitchhike* referred to Ride & Tie.

The Sport

Thus, Ride & Tie has its roots in historical necessity—survival and endurance. But its development as a modern sport must also be considered in terms of its relationship to the "sport of kings," or horse racing in general.

The first recorded account of horseback racing for purposes other than war is a description of Mohammed's use of the horse. He used the horse to spread word of his religion "to far places and in the fastest possible time before other horses could arrive."** The missionaries (travelling from West Africa to Mecca) were held in awe by those who had never seen the animal before, and many converts were made.

From that time until the fifteenth century, racehorses were bred only by kings and royalty. English royalty began racing horses to see which ones were best. These horses, Arabians, competed in four-mile races. Four miles was chosen

---

*Ann McGovern, *If You Lived in Colonial Times* (New York: Scholastic Book Service, 1964), pp. 61-62.

**Frank G. Menke, *Encyclopedia of Sports* (New York: A. L. Barnes, & Co., 1963), p. 527.

as the standard race length, since this had been the standard for the chariot races of the Olympian Games fifteen centuries earlier.

By the early 1700s, horse racing had become popular all over Europe, and on the American continent as well. Horses bred in America, however, were not yet comparable to those bred in England. Therefore, in American horse races rules were made to confine competitors to horses bred in America. But in spite of the rules, English "ringers" were still entered, and it was up to American ingenuity to even the odds.

It was at this point that the endurance factor was introduced to horse racing. Americans preferred to match the hardiness of their horses to the speed of the European horses. In one such race, first place was determined by the distance covered by each horse before one or the other dropped dead. Although more humane considerations followed, endurance-type racing was here to stay.

There is no doubt that Ride & Tie is an offshoot of endurance racing. But in Ride & Tie man and horse compete in a manner more demanding than traditional endurance riding. Although endurance riding requires a high level of equestrian skills, the physical and mental challenge to the rider does not compare to that met by the Ride & Tie competitor. In this regard, Ride & Tie may be more similar to the American rodeo, where challenges to the rider often call on a high degree of physical skill and prowess.

Perhaps it was this relationship between the rodeo cowboy and his horse that inspired Bud Johns with the idea of a Ride & Tie race. During his thirty years experience as a sportswriter and newspaperman he had covered many rodeo events. He gained a deep respect for the courage, dedication, determination, and skill displayed by rodeo athletes. He admired the teamwork between horse and man, and savored the natural ruggedness of the various events. These were the ingredients that would eventually blend into the making of the Ride & Tie.

Bud Johns, a tall, pipe-toting gentleman with a rough, gray beard that looks years older than his straight brown head of hair, appears at first sight to be better suited to riding shotgun on an overland stage than sitting behind a desk in a plush executive office building. However, when Bud was hired as public relations man for Levi Strauss in 1969, he knew exactly what he was up to. In less than two years he managed to organize the most unique promotional event the company had ever seen. Within the short span of seven years, Ride & Tie has been the subject of feature articles in *Sports Illustrated, Newsweek, True, Runner's World, Saddle Action, WomenSports,* and many other notable publications.

Bud Johns first conceived of the idea of a Ride & Tie race while researching some old newspaper clippings. One article, printed in the *San Diego Union* on July 23, 1933, described an 1874 horse-stealing episode that had occurred in Pine Valley, California. The article quoted the recollections of a Mr. C. F. Emery about how he and his father covered forty miles of "wild, secluded" terrain in order to recover their stolen horses. The paragraph that caught Bud's eye read as follows:

> We had only the one horse which could be ridden, so father and I started for San Diego, "ride and tie." That is, one started riding, the other walking. The rider, after covering a suitable distance, would tie the horse and proceed on foot. The other, on reaching the horse, would mount, ride past the walker and repeat the procedure. In this manner we covered about 40 miles in a day, bringing us about to the present site of La Mesa. This distance easily could be covered in an hour by auto now.

When Bud presented the idea to the Levi Strauss staff, it was approved without much difficulty. Although no one could imagine exactly what would transpire in such a race, the idea seemed better matched to the rugged image of the Levi Strauss product than a golf or tennis tournament. Levi was already successfully involved in promotional work with rodeos, and the Ride & Tie idea seemed compatible with this direction. In fact, the Rodeo Cowboys Association was even a bit worried that the event might compete with the rodeo. As it turned out, very few rodeo cowboys were willing to take on the long-distance running challenge of the Ride & Tie.

Two exceptions to this, however, were rodeo champions Bob Ragsdale and Jerry Koile. Not only were they anxious to take on the event, but both ran as a regular part of their conditioning program. Admittedly, both professional rodeo cowboys were after the $3,575 first-prize money. But as we shall see throughout this book, no one competes in a Ride & Tie race just for the money.

The first Levi's Ride & Tie race was held in California's Sonoma County. The race was advertised in various horseman's magazines and attracted fifty-nine two-rider, one-horse teams. The participants included schoolteachers, students, fire fighters, and housewives. Most were horse-people, many were competitive endurance riders, and some were runners. There were even several teams from the 10th Cavalry "Buffalo Soldiers," a group of black stunt men and actors from Hollywood.

The course consisted of over twenty-eight miles of rugged, canyon country. The temperature was in the eighties, and grades were as steep as 2,000 feet in three linear miles. Each team was required to tie its horse and switch riders at least four times. Prizes were given to the first team overall, the first man-woman team, and the first two-woman team. Three hours and forty-eight minutes after the start, twenty-two-year-old Jim Larimer and sixteen-year-old Hal Hall became the first National Ride & Tie champions. Both were experienced endurance riders and high school athletes. They had been asked to compete in the event by the owner of a six-year-old thoroughbred, the third member of the winning team. The owner had seen the young men leading their horses up steep hills with no apparent strain in endurance rides, and figured they would have a good chance with her horse Tabby. The team stayed in front the entire race.

Others were not so fortunate. Ragsdale and Koile had been in good position until their horse slipped down a forty-foot embankment. They finished sixth. Other contestants strayed off trails and went miles out of the way. Two horses did not make it at all; they died from exhaustion. It is important from the standpoint of the sport's development to understand the implications of the deaths of the two horses in the first Ride & Tie. The original planning of the race had placed a high priority on safeguarding the animals' health. Veterinarians were hired to examine the horses both before the race and at a ten-mile Vet Check. Although standard endurance riding precautions were exercised, such precautions were unfortunately not extensive enough. It must be remembered

that never before in the history of modern horse racing had
there been such a race as Ride & Tie. No one could have
known what demands would be placed on horses being ridden under such conditions. First of all, there was the rugged
terrain. Never before had such a terrain been encountered by
a racehorse. Some trails were no more than deer trails, winding up and down steep canyons. In some areas, loose rocks
made footing difficult. In others, thick chaparral virtually covered the trail. Then, there was the fact that two different riders were responsible for pacing the horse. Furthermore, traditional endurance competition did not involve the pressure to
catch up or the stop-and-go procedure. The participating veterinarians simply did not know what the horses were up
against. Nor did the riders.

This tragic experience, however, made a significant contribution to the future of the sport. It was an obstacle that, because it was overcome, gave permanence to Ride & Tie. In
spite of threats to end the sport forever, the sponsors, the
contestants, and the veterinarians were convinced that such
problems could be avoided in future Ride & Ties. In later
races, highly qualified vet teams would conduct stringent examinations of the horses' conditions before, during, and after
the race. By the time of the second annual Ride & Tie, a new
awareness of the capabilities of the horse had been born.
Equine physiology and stress factors were examined on a new
plateau. The distinguished veterinarian, Dr. James Steere, who
participated in the first Ride & Tie, stated afterward that it
was the first time he truly understood the horse. From that
point on, he became instrumental in helping assure that horses
would not be allowed to continue beyond their individual
limits. Such measures would safeguard future Ride & Tie
horses, while increasing the challenge to the rider.

The Philosophy

Thus far we have seen that the development of Ride & Tie
is related to historic nostalgia, horse racing popularity, American tradition, and the enthusiasm and dedication of the pro-
moters and participants of the first race. But perhaps more
than any of these factors, the growing appeal of Ride & Tie is

related to the basic nature of modern man. It has given men and women an opportunity to experience their natural potential. It affords the opportunity to understand the significance of survival, the meaning of courage, the satisfaction of achievement, and the joy of play, in spite of the stifling artificiality of modern civilization. Participation in Ride & Tie can rekindle the warmth of human contact with nature, with one another, and with ourselves. Through these things we are better able to understand our relationship with our world. The appeal of Ride & Tie is thus an answer to "the call of the wild."

Sports have been created to provide this outlet. Sports have attempted to simulate our all but lost natural environment and its intrinsic challenges. Few sports, however, come as close to recreating the holistic challenge as Ride & Tie. Ride & Tie seems to duplicate the natural processes of life that have long called upon our fundamental drives. Such processes include an involvement with wilderness, and an emphasis on the need to endure rather than to conquer.

Such philosophical considerations may be significant. As civilization and technology draw man away from his natural environment, his very existence becomes threatened unless he maintains the integrity of his own nature. A good example is our nation's increasing mental health problem and hypokinetic disease. Inactivity, the most flagrant enemy of human potential, is threatening society more than any other technological waste product. Inactivity is antithetical to Ride & Tie. Activity is inherent to man's ability to survive. It has been a constant in man's nature from primitive to modern societies. Where once human activity provided food, shelter, and protection, it now must save us from physical deterioration and mental depression. Assuming mental and physical activity is basic to man's ability to express his full potential, it must be intense enough to propel one toward one's potential. If primitive man did not push himself to his limits, he would have starved or been eaten by some predator. Today man's activity level must likewise be sufficient if he is to survive. The only difference is that in modern times we must invent an outlet for such activity.

Jumping over creeks, keeping your shoes dry, is part of the Ride & Tie challenge. (Scotty Ray Morris)

Involvement with nature has long been a motive for participation in sports. Mountain climbing, river rafting, and backpacking are but a few examples of popular sports that bring us into contact with the wilderness. Proximity with wilderness in Ride & Tie, however, has a special significance. Not only is there the rugged wilderness environment, but there is also an involvement with an animal of the wilderness, *Equus caballus. Equus caballus* (the horse) is one of the oldest animals. In one form or another the horse dates back 45 million years. Although most horses are no longer creatures of the wilderness, they have remained wild animals in spite of domestication. Even the best-trained horse retains its instinctive awareness and desire to run free. On a challenging course and amidst the anxiety of competition, the horse can become a formidable creature. The relationship between man and horse can be a harmonious confrontation with the raw and unpredictable elements of nature. It is also a reunion with an animal with whom we share a similar roaming ancestry.

Not only does intimacy with wilderness make Ride & Tie an appealing sport, but the emphasis on enduring rather than winning has also encouraged the sport's development. Although there is a fine line between these two terms, their difference is important. People are finding an increasing need to apply the old adage, "It's not whether you win or lose but how you play the game." Many people now view the concepts of victory and defeat as further contributing to society's dehumanization of the individual. People are looking for a way to test themselves to the limit without having to win or lose.

In modern distance and cross-country running, many participants compete only against themselves. Even in many competitive races, runners may be more concerned with their time than whether or not they are the first across the finish line. This concern over the more intrinsic qualities of competitive running seems to increase with the difficulty and challenge of the run. In the marathon, which is considered the ultimate race, participants have enough to contend with without worrying about the performance of someone else.

Distance running may be the answer, in view of the fact that it is the nation's fastest growing sport. Distance running, like horseback riding, recalls an activity that once enhanced man's ability to survive. Running is perhaps the most basic of man's natural capabilities. In ancient days man's ability to run was probably correlated closely with his ability to survive: he ran to catch food; he ran from danger; he ran for shelter; and perhaps he ran for pleasure.

But now there is a new ultimate endurance race—one that incorporates all of the characteristics that many of us have been seeking and most of us need. In Ride & Tie everyone who tries is a winner. As in most of life, the outcome of the race is dependent on all the variables from skill to chance. Walt Schafer, winner of the Brown's Ride & Tie and a participant in the Levi's Ride & Tie, calls the race a "living drama, with the rewards and disappointments of life." Schafer, a thirty-eight-year-old professor, has been running cross-country for twenty-four years. He runs a 2:37 marathon and competed on a world record relay team. In spite of the many challenges of his career, he says that the first four miles of Ride & Tie were the most exciting thing he has ever done, the next thirty-odd were the toughest, and the last mile the most rewarding.

Thus, the successful development of Ride & Tie racing represents the culmination of many factors—from the history of transportation and man's relationship to the horse to professional promotion and the merger of two popular sports. But most important, Ride & Tie affords an ideal opportunity for us to express our full positive potentialities. It has grown because such opportunities are becoming rare in our world. It will remain as long as we remember our history. The important thing is not winning but taking part. "The essential thing in life is not conquering but fighting well."* This is what Ride & Tie is all about.

*"The Olympic Creed," by Baron Pierre de Coubertin.

Part Two
The Runner

3

Training the Runner

*In running, the body is an audience
to its own performance. As such, the
show business adage applies: "Always
leave the audience wanting more."*

Although you may prefer to begin your training emphasis on riding, this book will concentrate first on running.
Even if you are already an accomplished runner, it may be
helpful to adapt your training methods to those prescribed
here before proceeding to the chapters on riding and care of
the horse. By so doing you will accomplish two things: (1)
you will be better able to cope physically with the combined
training for riding and running; and (2) by concentrating on
running first, your understanding of the horse will improve,
since your endurance needs are similar in many ways to those
of the horse.

From the Ground Up

Our first item of concern, the running shoe, represents the
most important consideration in training—preventive maintenance. The prevention of illness and injury will have top priority in our training program. Since many running injuries
originate at the foot, we begin by focusing on proper footwear. (Training the horse requires similar considerations.)

Originally, shoes were as foreign to humans as they were to
horses. However, as man moved to new environments and in-
vented new forms of transportation, shoes became a necessity. Technology brought with it broken glass and concrete.
Eventually, social morality took over and nakedness became
improper.

Shoes were originally designed with little thought to pre-
serving the natural functioning of the foot. With the modern

transportation (beginning with the horse), man has travelled by foot less and less. As a result our feet have become soft, spoiled, and not as adequate for running as they might be. This, and the fact that evolution has proceeded slowly since our feet were hands, may be why many people exhibit foot abnormalities. For example, about 30 percent of the population has Morton's foot, in which the first toe is shorter than the second toe. Although the foot is structurally similar to the hand, the first toe evolved to be less mobile, larger, and more solid than the thumb. Since many running injuries are attributable to the first toe being too short, it is likely that centuries of relative inactivity have impeded this evolutionary development.

Fortunately, it is possible for us to rectify such problems. We have learned to design shoes and biomechanical devices that help put the foot in proper relation to the ground. By selecting the proper shoe, it is possible to avoid many problems relating to improper foot balance. When shopping, you should ask specifically for a running shoe or a training flat. Such a shoe should have a durable and well-cushioned sole that is still flexible and easy to bend. It should have a rigid shank support from the front of the arch to the heel. The shoe should have a firm heel counter that allows your heel to fit snugly, and a heel wedge that lifts the heel about a half-inch higher than the ball of the foot. It should also have a well formed, roomy toe box to allow natural toe spread. But most important of all, the shoe should feel comfortable! A shoe that is good for someone else may be bad for you.

It has been my experience that waffle-sole shoes are best for the loose, rocky hill terrain. Deep-ridged soles, with forward and reverse angles, are adequate for more compact hillsides. It is recommended that the firmer training shoe be used in Ride & Tie events, rather than the lighter racing flat.

Even if you have selected a good running shoe it is still possible they will seem inadequate once you do some running. If you suspect shoe problems are responsible for running pain or injury, it is time to begin experimenting. If you are having knee problems, for example, you might try arch supports. If your toenails are becoming damaged, you might try slitting the shoe in front of the toe. If the sole is too stiff you can make lengthwise cuts along the bottoms to make them more flexible. If the shoe is beginning to wear down, you can use a sole repair kit to alleviate some problems. You can add insoles to reduce shock. Or, you can buy a different pair of shoes.

Experimenting with new shoes, however, can become expensive. Remember, shoes are only one variable that may be responsible for your problems. If you do buy a second pair of shoes, hold onto the originals (if they are in good shape), as you may find you can return to them as your muscle balance, flexibility, strength, and running style progress. The need for proper shoes cannot be overemphasized. The aspiring Ride & Tie participant should be constantly aware of the condition of shoes and their effect on performance. Improper shoes can cause injuries to the foot, ankle, calf, knee, hip, and back. However, shoes are only one aspect of the preventive foot care. Equally important are conditioning and running technique. Foot strength and support can be improved through foot exercises.

The foot is a complex combination of muscle, bone, tendons, and ligaments. The most intricate anatomical structures are the arches, which help support the upright body. Even with normal feet and proper shoes, running injuries can occur if the muscles and ligaments supporting the arches are weak and inflexible. The most vulnerable area of the foot is near the middle of the longitudinal arch. This weak part of the arch is most prone to injury when the ligaments of the arch are overrelaxed. When such a condition exists, the arch can be flattened with the extreme pressure of running or leaping on or off your horse. The same problem can occur if you are overweight. Furthermore, Ride & Tie courses—usually full of holes and irregularities—can also put a strain on ligaments. But the ligaments and muscles of the foot can be strengthened. Since all the muscles of the foot help to control toe movement, simple toe exercises can help develop strength in the entire foot. Imagine that the entire foot is a hand, and attempt to make a fist with it. Then, open it as wide as possible. Raising and lowering the toes in this fashion for one or two minutes will help prepare the foot for those demanding runs along the rugged sloping hills of a Ride & Tie course.

Another way to condition the foot is by regularly running barefoot. The runs should be made on soft, grassy fields or on sand. Another alternative is to run around a cinder track wearing an old, heavy pair of socks. As with any new training technique, barefoot runs should begin gradually and be of short duration. These runs will both strengthen and rejuvenate the foot. After a long cross-country run, you may want to cool down the final quarter-mile by taking off your shoes and socks and gently walking to the finish. The massaging action of the terrain on the tired foot is therapeutic and refreshing.

Simple foot care is also an important preventive measure. Your feet should be clean and dry before a run. Your toenails should be cut straight across and the cuticles should be pushed back. If your feet become sore, you should massage them and soak them in warm water. You should examine feet for the onset of blisters or calluses. If a blister occurs, it is important to keep it clean and tape it before another run.

Prevention of blisters is an important consideration for Ride & Tie participants, since they are more likely to occur on this type of terrain. When running down steep hills, the foot is subject to more abrasive action, thus causing hot spots that can become blisters. Most Ride & Tiers wear one or two pairs of socks to prevent blisters. If you wear socks, make sure they are thick, dry, and clean. If you do not wear socks it is a good idea to powder your feet to decrease perspiration and rubbing. If you notice a friction spot, a liberal dose of Vaseline on the foot may help.

A final consideration has to do with foot strike during running. Proper foot plant can prevent injuries, not only to the foot, but to the entire kinetic chain up to the lower back. Foot plant in cross-country running should be similar to that of walking, with the exception of sprinting and uphill running. This is because in walking, the foot lands naturally, starting with the heel, moving along the outside edge, and coming up off the pads of the toes. In running, this motion is not exaggerated, but is subtle so that the foot seems to land flat. Such placement of the foot is in harmony with its structure. The line of the foot, from the point of the heel to the toes, is not quite straight, but is directed a little outward. The inner border of the foot is a little convex, while the outer border is concave. The inner border of the central portion of the longitudinal arch is thus slightly elevated; from this point the bones arch over to the outer border. It is this outer portion that is in closest contact with the ground. This structure allows the foot to spread the impact of the body's weight with a continual movement rather than a sudden stop. Since the body weight on each foot triples during running, it is especially important to maintain this motion in training and racing.

As in walking, the body should remain upright in cross-country running. Since the human foot is at right angles to the leg (unlike the horse, whose hooves are at 45 degree angles), foot strike should occur directly beneth the knee. You can imagine a perpendicular line running from the ground through the heel, up the lower leg, past the hip, and out the shoulder. In order to adapt this foot plant to running, the foot must be on its way back before the heel actually touches the ground. The foot should land straight forward, the buttocks should be comfortably tucked under, and the head should be balanced and square. It helps me to imagine a cable attached to my navel, parallel to the ground, that pulls me continually forward.

It has been demonstrated in research at the University of Illinois that proper foot angle can prevent injuries. The research, conducted by William F. Leach, Ph.D., showed that runners who were not prone to shin splints landed on the ground with the foot in line with the knee and hip. Runners prone to shin splints landed with a greater degree of angle.*

The reference to walking in our preventive maintenance discussion has a twofold purpose. Not only does it help to develop proper running technique, but it also provides an alternate training and racing pace that is advantageous during periods of excessive stress or fatigue. I refer here to "race walking" and its swivel-hipped, knee locking motion. With such a motion there is little impact shock on the body and it should be relied on when you are at the threshold of pain in such areas as the knee or lower back. By so doing, the therapeutic effect may be enough to allow you to return to an improved, pain-

---

*Dr. George Sheehan, *Encyclopedia of Athletic Medicine* (Mountain View, Calif.: World Publications, 1972), p. 43.

free running motion before you compound the injury to a more permanent disposition.

A member of one team competing in a Ride & Tie event race-walked the entire time he was on foot. On the steep downhills he was consistent in his pace and well balanced. On the steep uphill climbs he "elephant walked" past more than one struggling runner. On the flat stretches of terrain he looked much less sensible but he seemed to be able to mount his horse with less effort than others in the final stages of the game. And his team did finish the race in a respectable position. He also probably danced the socks off of everyone at the awards ceremony!

If none of your experimentation seems to work, and if you are doing everything else right, then it is time to see a sports podiatrist, preferably one who is a runner himself. The podiatrist can help pinpoint the specific problem and can recommend an appropriate solution. It should be remembered, however, that in most cases the problem is structural, not medical. Dr. Harry Hlavac, a runner and founder of the Sports Medicine Clinic at the California College of Podiatric Medicine in San Francisco, has published remedial guidelines in a pamphlet entitled, *Good Shoes for Bad Feet:* *

> Relief from Achilles tendonitis needs a flexible shoe with cushioning of the bottom of the heel and good elevation. Ankle sprains and instability need a shoe that will provide support and balance at heel contact. Arch problems and flexible flat feet require shoes that have a good shank and conforming arch. Calluses on the bottom of the foot require a deep toe box, proper fit, and no pressure from "stretch socks." Problems in the back of the heel usually require cupping and elevation, while problems at the bottom of the heel (heel spurs, bruises, plantar fascitis, "joggers heel"), require all of those plus flexible cushioning. Forefoot pain or metatarsalgia, whether caused by forefoot imbalance, stone bruises, neuritis or lack of normal protective fat padding will be helped by thick, but flexible cushioning.

Proper concern for the feet before going full stride into running can prevent many problems. Similarly, prerun training and exercises for the remainder of the body can significantly increase the possibility of reaching your full potential without suffering setbacks caused by injury and fatigue. Con-

---

*Dr. Harry Hlavac, *Good Shoes for Bad Feet* (San Francisco, 1975), self-published.

ditioning through running and riding alone will not protect you against such setbacks. The proper combination of stretching and strengthening exercises will better protect you.

The activities for which we are training are not enough to prepare us against injury because they do not consistently demand abnormal muscular responses such as cause injury. It is the running accidents that cause inhibiting strains and sprains to the muscles and ligaments from the foot to the back. It is the unexpected movements of the horse that cause injuries to the arms, shoulders, and neck. If a boxer trained only by boxing it is most likely that he would be lacking the strength and resilience to survive a well-conditioned opponent.

SILK

Since fitness can only be obtained with gradual and regular exposure to stress, muscles must be strengthened and stretched to levels not normally encountered in running and riding. The requirement is to both strengthen and stretch the muscles. In the well-conditioned individual, suppleness and strength are inseparable kinesthetic ingredients. I call such conditioning one's *SILK*, or *strong and inherently lithe kinesthesia*, or strong and inseparably supple muscle sense.

SILK also refers to the "muscle sense" of the cardiovascular system. The fibers of the heart muscle and blood vessels also need to be strong and elastic. Cardiovascular fitness should be a prerequisite for safe and confident training, although this system will improve with actual running and riding. This confidence, an important Ride & Tie ingredient, is gained with the attainment of SILK. Control of the horse is related to the amount of confidence displayed by the rider. Equally important, however, is the occasional need for decisive, confident reactions when unexpected situations occur. For example, one afternoon I was training an Arabian horse to run with only a rope halter. Coming over the crest of a hill, the horse suddenly lurched into a fast run and headed toward a large, low-hanging branch. My efforts to turn or slow down the animal only excited him more and increased his pace. The branch was almost low enough to scrape the top of the saddle and I knew that merely ducking would not suffice, nor did jumping off seem a safe alternative. Instead I elected to swing off to the side of the horse, holding on with one foot in the stirrup and a death grip on the mane. When we passed the branch I pulled myself back onto the saddle and continued my attempt to calm and slow the horse. As we approached a small hill he slowed down, whether in response to the steep incline or my efforts I don't know. I had but a moment to make my move before his pace quickened at the crest of the hill. Once again I swung off the side of the horse, this time landing on the ground, balancing and setting myself until I was able to jerk his head around with the lead rope.

I do not mean to digress to extreme examples of horsemanship, but the fact remains that had I not been confident in the overall strength and flexibility of my body I would probably have hit the branch. Without lithe muscles and flexibility I would not have been able to achieve the range of motion necessary to avoid the branch. Without strength I would not have been able to pull myself back in the saddle or later pull the horse to a halt. The move went "smooth as silk" because I had my SILK.

Performance objectives should be limited to existing levels of strength and flexibility. This rule should apply throughout the training program. In order to help you measure your overall conditioning, I have included several physiological measurements to serve as guidelines to measure your SILK progress, and establish performance objectives. These measurements, based on surmised and actual conclusions of extensive research, can be found in Appendix I at the back of the book.* Measurements, a chart for studying progress, and a "step test" for determining overall conditioning are all included in Appendix II.

Developing a Training Chart

In order to be effective, these measurements need to be incorporated into an overall training program. Results should be obtained and recorded from the beginning. Organization is the

---

*The research includes laboratory and field testing of 100 fire fighters from Washington, D.C., who were tested extensively with established protocols. See "Development of a Job-Related Physical Performance Examination for Firefighters," (National Fire Protection Association, U.S. Department of Commerce, Washington, D. C., 1975).

prerequisite for this initial stage of Ride & Tie preparation. Beginning and experienced runners can benefit from a daily schedule listing objectives, accomplishments, physiological measurements, injuries, and psychological considerations of the training activities. Such a schedule can be an invaluable guide for learning how your body is responding to various training techniques, and may keep you from overlooking important aspects of training. It can also provide a significant source of motivation to continue the training. Although you may want to design your own form of record-keeping, a sample chart offering several advantages has been included. The chart combines an entire month's training entries on one page, allowing more convenient analysis and comparison. It is designed to guide the beginning Ride & Tier toward a preliminary measure of SILK sufficient to begin the more stringent aspects of training. The chart also can be used to make entries referring to more advanced runs, and can be improvised to include conditioning of the horse.

At the "heart" of the training chart is the heart itself. The heart is responsible for the power, the longevity, and the dependability of the human body. The performance efficiency of the heart is easy to measure. These measurements will be the primary concern for those entering the first stage of Ride & Tie training.

At this point, most fitness texts would precaution the reader to see a doctor before beginning the exercise program. Unfortunately, I think such "warnings" have done more to curtail health than promote it. The precaution should be directed more toward what will happen to you if you don't begin exercising. I believe that most of the medical profession is more familiar with illness than health, and a visit to your doctor may not be very helpful. Ask for a stress test. But, because of legal problems, lack of training and equipment, and expense many doctors will deny the request. And all a standard exam, without a stress test, will tell you is that you'll be all right as long as you remain inactive. Although the medical profession is still far behind in the area of preventive medicine, there are a growing number of exceptions. If these facilities or individuals are available to you, it cannot hurt to take advantage of them. Although gradual exercise based on your target heart

TABLE 1
Training Chart

Name _____   Month _____ 19 ____

Heart Rate Requirements: Lower Limit _____ beats per minute

                             Upper Limit _____ beats per minute   Target Rate _____

                             (Exercise Session Measurements)

Date	Resting Pulse (upon arising)	Midway Pulse Rate	Pulse Rate at Completion	Two-minute Recovery Pulse Rate	Description of Exercise, Course, Time, Diet, etc.
1					
2					
3					
4					
5					
6					
7					
8					
9					
10					
11					
12					
13					
14					
15					
16					
17					

| 18 |
| 19 |
| 20 |
| 21 |
| 22 |
| 23 |
| 24 |
| 25 |
| 26 |
| 27 |
| 28 |
| 29 |
| 30 |
| 31 |

Monthly Progress Record

Description	Resting Pulse Rate	Age-Adj. Score	Strength/Flexibility Score	SILK Rating	Recommended Weekly Mileage
Start of Training					
End of Last Month					
End of This Month					

Comments reflecting entire month's training:

rate and other considerations described in this book should make exercise safe for almost everyone, it is true that about 20 percent of heart attacks in males over the age of thirty-five are asymptomatic. Thus, an exercise electrocardiogram (EKG) and body chemistry profile could be helpful in providing you with a more exact exercise prescription than the approximations given here. Although abnormalities might be discovered that would dictate a higher degree of precaution, the profiles should primarily be used for annual lifelong comparisons. As for Ride & Tie, let your heart and chart lead the way.

Near the top of the chart, where it reads, "Heart Rate Requirements," there are two blanks entitled "Lower Limit" and "Upper Limit." These blanks will describe the limits of your *target zone* heart rate. This is the rate at which your heart must function during exercise in order to achieve safe and improved performance efficiency. Working at a rate less than the lower limit will not cause significant improvement and working above the upper limit may cause unsafe, over-exertion conditions. For our purposes in the beginning stage of training, heart rates should remain in the bottom half of the target zone during the exercise session.

The target zone has been determined by taking a percentage of an individual's maximum *aerobic* capacity.* Maximum aerobic capacity describes the maximum amount of oxygen the heart can deliver to working muscles. At this point the heart cannot beat any faster and the muscles run out of fuel to continue the work. By exercising the heart muscle at a rate within the target zone, this point can be delayed so that more work can be performed before exhaustion occurs. This is accomplished by strengthening the heart muscle so it is able to furnish more oxygenated blood to the muscles with one beat than it could previously furnish with several beats.

It is the heart rate that becomes our measure of success. By regularly putting a demand on the heart that causes it to beat within 70 and 85 percent of its maximum rate, we can eventually reduce the number of beats required to maintain a

*Aerobic refers to exercise within one's capacity to use oxygen. *An-aerobic*, converesly, relates to vigorous exercise at a rate beyond the body's ability to obtain oxygen. This creates *oxygen debt*. Anaerobic exercise is not conducive to exercise goals such as endurance, fat loss, or feeling of well-being.

specific work load. In order to determine your average maximum attainable heart rate, simply subtract your age from the number 220. In the blank on the chart enter your "lower limit," which is 70 percent of the remainder (220 minus age times 0.70). In the blank for the "upper limit" enter the number that is 85 percent of the remainder (220 minus age times 0.85). It is important to use the bottom half of the range as your target if you are just beginning an exercise program because these are only averages. Another way to determine your approximate "ideal" training pulse rate is to take 70 percent of the difference between the resting pulse rate (R.P.R.) and the maximal pulse rate (determined by subtracting your age from 220), then adding the resting pulse rate to that product (220 minus age minus R.P.R. times 0.70 R.P.R.).*

You should become expert at taking your own pulse to determine if you are in the target zone during exercise. You should monitor your pulse rate before and after exercise. Since the pulse count is the same as the heart rate, you can determine the number of beats per minute by merely placing your hand over your heart. The easiest place to locate the pulse, however, is at the radial artery located on the underside of the wrist below the thumb joint. Just place your first and second fingers over the area and count the number of beats felt in six seconds and multiply by ten. This formula is a closer approximation than the standard fifteen second count multiplied by four because the heart rate begins to slow immediately following the end of exercise movement.

Team Training Schedule

The chart has been designed to help you organize your team's training schedule. It is intended for use during the six months prior to race time. The individual training program is twelve months long, so you should have achieved a good physical fitness base before starting on this comprehensive schedule. Furthermore, the mileage recommended on this chart should be achieved only if compatable with your individual scores on the SILK chart.

*If you know your average resting pulse rate (standing), this formula, known as the Karvonan formula, is slightly more accurate. Your upper and lower limits can be determined using 60 and 80 percent instead of 70 percent.

TABLE 2
Six-Month Team Training Schedule
Use in conjunction with SILK Chart

A designates one teammate
B designates other teammate

January

		Mon.	Tues.	Wed.	Thurs.	Fri.	Sat.*	Sun.	Total Individual Weekly Running Mileage			
									1st wk.	2nd wk.	3rd wk.	4th wk.
Running	A	6		8	6		10		42	42	42	42
	B	6	6	8			10		42	42	42	42
Riding	A		8						20	20	20	20
	B				8				20	20	20	20
Ride & Tie**						10		14	24	24	24	24

Weekly mileage for horse: 50

February

		Mon.	Tues.	Wed.	Thurs.	Fri.	Sat.*	Sun.	Total Individual Weekly Running Mileage			
									1st wk.	2nd wk.	3rd wk.	4th wk.
Running	A	6		8	8		10		45	45	45	Add 1
	B	6	8	8			10		45	45	45	Add 1
Riding	A		8						21	21	21	Add 1
	B				8				21	21	21	Add 1
Ride & Tie						12		14	26	26	26	Add 1

Weekly mileage for horse: 52

March

		Mon.	Tues.	Wed.	Thurs.	Fri.	Sat.*	Sun.	Total Individual Weekly Running Mileage			
									1st wk.	2nd wk.	3rd wk.	4th wk.
Running	A	8		10	10		12		57	57	57	57
	B	8	10	10			12		57	57	57	57
Riding	A		10						27	27	27	27
	B				10				27	27	27	27
Ride & Tie						14		20	34	34	34	34

Weekly mileage for horse: 66

April

	Mon.	Tues.	Wed.	Thurs.	Fri.	Sat.*	Sun.	1st wk.	2nd wk.	3rd wk.	4th wk.
Running A	10			10		15		69	69	69	69
Running B	10	10	12			15		69	69	69	69
Riding A		12						34	34	34	34
Riding B			12	12				34	34	34	34
Ride & Tie					20		24	44	44	44	44

Weekly mileage for horse: 83

May

	Mon.	Tues.	Wed.	Thurs.	Fri.	Sat.*	Sun.	1st wk.	2nd wk.	3rd wk.	4th wk.
Running A	10			10		20		80	80	80	80
Running B	10	10	15			20		80	80	80	80
Riding A		15						40	40	40	40
Riding B			15	15				40	40	40	40
Ride & Tie					20		30	50	50	50	50

Weekly mileage for horse: 100

June

	Mon.	Tues.	Wed.	Thurs.	Fri.	Sat.*	Sun.	1st wk.	2nd wk.	3rd wk.	4th wk.
Running A	10			10		20		80	69	69	69
Running B	10	10	15			20		80	69	69	69
Riding A		15						40	34	34	34
Riding B			15	15				40	34	34	34
Ride & Tie					20		30	50	44	44	44

* "Pony" horse alongside for Saturday runs (halter—no saddle).

** Entire team. For mileage, figure each person runs about ½ total distance in box.

It should be noted that total running mileage for the week is a combination of miles run during running training alone and during Ride & Tie sessions. Total riding mileage is a combination of riding training alone and Ride & Tie sessions. During Ride & Tie it is assumed that you will be running half the total distance and riding the other half. To determine the amount of miles the horse will be running, use the total mileage figure from Ride & Tie sessions, riding sessions, and Saturday running sessions, during which the horse will run alongside you.

Once you have determined your target zone, you know the intensity at which you must exercise in order to make progress. In our first stage of training the duration of exercise can be a minimum of twenty minutes done four times a week. This is twenty minutes at the target zone and does not include the stretching and strengthening exercises to be described later. The type of exercise used for this twenty minutes can vary, but you should remain with it for the first two or three months of our twelve-month training period. (Yes, I said twelve months! Did you think you were going to prepare for the "toughest game" in a month?)

My first choice for the target zone exercise session, for the beginning runner or nonrunning endurance rider, is race walking. Try to find a twenty-minute course that includes some inclines. With slight inclines you will not have to overexaggerate the form in order to get your pulse rate up. Ideally, you will spend the twenty or thirty minutes hiking in the woods, on fire roads, or on hilly terrain. Whatever route you take, be sure to take your pulse midway to be sure you are at your target zone. My second choice for the session is use of a stationary ergometer, such as an exercycle, rowing machine, or treadmill. A bicycle is all right too, but city riding makes it difficult to keep up the heart rate. The third suggestion is a wooden box or bench that measures 15¾ inches high. The box should be sturdy enough to step up and down on safely. The exact measurement of the box is important because it can be reused for the SILK measurements. My final recommended alternative is rope skipping. It is important that you skip with a four-beat rhythm to minimize concentrated foot compressions. It is best to jump on a spongy surface, such as a rubber mat.

The beginning runner may wonder why running is not one of the recommended beginning exercises. It is because we are trying to reduce the beginning runners' attrition rate. You will be better prepared to run without injury by gradually attaining a degree of SILK before actually running. Also, there may be an incentive to save the running experience as something special and fun in comparison to the initial chore of becoming physically fit. Depending on your present condition, you should be able to transfer to running in approximately one or two months. Improvements in physical fitness are most dramatic at the beginning of a training program and you should be able to achieve the recommended prerun SILK measurements in a short period of time.

Stretching Exercises

The SILK rating should be entered monthly on your training chart along with the recommended weekly mileage. In order to improve this score continually you must do strengthening and stretching exercises every day, preferably both before and after target zone training. As for particular exercises, I have included a few that have been successful. There are, however, many other effective exercises. I suggest that you experiment in order to find the ones that suit you best. The important thing is not to miss any area. A good rule to follow is to stretch and strengthen any muscle and its opposing muscle. Deciding which muscles to exercise will also increase interest and awareness about your training program.

The exercise I recommend doing first is called the "Frankenstein Toe Balance." This exercise consists of merely closing your eyes while standing with your arms outstretched in front, and rising up on your toes as high as possible. The goal is to hold this position without falling off your toes or losing your balance for one full minute. The exercise improves the balance reflexes pertaining to the gastrocnemius, the adductor magnus, the gluteus maximum and the back extensors. It also is a good beginning exercise as it focuses your concentration on your body without strenuous effort. This makes getting started a little easier.

The second exercise I call the "Dog Stretch." This one stretches and strengthens the lower back and should be done before and after the target zone work. You begin the exercise on your hands and knees. Then, lifting one knee upward and lowering the head, you should attempt to touch your nose to your knee in a slow, gradual stretching motion. After you have brought the knee up as high as you can, lift the head up and straighten the same leg out behind you as high as possible. From this position bend your elbows until your nose touches the floor. Repeat the cycle three times with each leg.

Prevention of disabling pain and injury to the spine is the primary reason for back and abdominal exercises. Unfortunately, participation in Ride & Tie competition and training can be conducive to such problems if you are not prepared. Ride & Tie can involve the three most responsible factors for lower back pain—exhaustion, extended contraction of anti-gravity muscles, and running over rough, uneven terrain.

These factors can all cause a hyperextension of the spine causing the column of disks to bulge forward and pinch the nerves that carry messages and regulate pain. Unless the muscles and ligaments that support the spine are flexible and strong, they cannot prevent the spine from being bent in this way. Not only is it necessary to maintain these supportive structures with exercise, but take care to maintain the position of the spine through correct posture as well. This includes posture during sitting, sleeping, running, and riding.

Correct posture for the spine is any position that keeps the lower back from curving or arching forward. Just as weak abdominal muscles allow the lower back to sag forward, sleeping incorrectly can cause swayback or lordosis of the spine. Your mattress should not be sagging. When you sleep, remain on your side with your knees tucked up in a fetal position, thus maintaining a safe position for the lower spine. Note that the neck portion of the spine is shaped similarly to the lower spine and should be treated accordingly.

When you are sitting for long periods of time you should always have at least one knee higher than your hips. This will help maintain a correct spinal position. Slouching in a chair all day can almost neutralize your stretching efforts during training. If you must stand for long hours during your work, you should periodically relax the tension on your anti-gravity torso muscles by kneeling down and resting your buttocks on the heel of one foot.

The final consideration of posture in preventing back problems is while running. By neither bending too far forward nor arching your shoulders too far backward, you will be able to keep your disks on top of one another where they belong. This will not only help prevent back pain but it will also improve your balance and allow you to run smoothly.

To continue with our exercises, you should incorporate "bent-knee leg raises" or "hanging leg raises" into your warm-up and your post-target zone. Bent-knee leg raises are accomplished by lifting your knee to your chest while in a prone position, then continuing until your toes are touching the floor behind your head. Then return to the floor and repeat. Another alternative is to hang on a pull-up bar and raise your knees to your chest until you are strong enough to raise them straight legged.

The spine also should be stretched laterally. To do this stretch, attempt to maintain the same hip position while twisting your trunk as far as possible, first to the left and then to the right. This will stretch the lateral supports of the spine and should be done whenever possible when sitting throughout the day.

Bent-knee sit-ups should be done regularly to strengthen the torso muscles and give good support to the spine. In order to avoid shortening the hip flexors during training, it is important to keep the knees bent. You can keep your arms crossed in front of you at first and as you become stronger you can place your hands behind your head. Since the abdominal muscles are primarily holding muscles, it is beneficial to hold a static contraction about halfway back for about ten seconds after every five sit-ups.

Leg Stretching. After completing the torso stretching and strengthening exercises, you should concentrate on stretching the legs. It should be remembered that running will shorten or contract those muscles that are primarily used during running. Although they are becoming stronger they are also becoming shorter and pulling against their attachments. A sudden increase in pace or change in terrain can thus result in a pulled muscle. By applying the SILK principle we can prevent such injuries.

Sit-ups, in any form, are important for strengthening muscles and improving breathing capabilities. (Greg Jennings)

The stretching exercise will increase the flexibility of the calf muscles. As with all stretching exercises it should be done slowly and gradually without a bouncing motion. This is especially important when it is being used as a warm-up before target zone work when muscles and ligaments are tightest. To begin, assume a modified push-up position except with feet flat and closer to your palms, with your buttocks higher than your back. Now, bring your head back toward your knees, with knees locked, and concentrate on stretching your calves. (Concentrating on the area you are trying to strengthen or stretch is more effective than doing the same exercise without the concentration.) As flexibility improves, begin to walk your hands back toward your feet keeping knees locked and feet flat.

I call this exercise a "*V*-stretch." It is excellent for stretching the upper calf muscles. To stretch the lower calf, stand in a position where the heel is lower than the toe and apply pressure or weight. This can be accomplished by standing with toes on a board or step and leaning forward until the hips are past the toes. You also can outstretch your leg while sitting down and pulling the sole of your foot back toward the shin to stretch this area. Once you know the feeling of the burning sensation in the calf you can experiment throughout the day with different ways to stretch.

The *V*-stretch. (Greg Jennings)

The importance of calf-stretching for Ride & Tie cannot be overemphasized. Statistics show that long-distance cross-country runners are most prone to injuries to calf muscles. Improving the flexibility of the calf will help prevent injuries (shin splints) to the anterior portion of the leg. This is because the shorter the calf muscle is, the harder the anterior muscles must work to raise the foot for proper foot plant during running. One muscle must work against another muscle because the body doesn't have its SILK. It should be noted that the calf stretches also will stretch the Achilles tendon, especially if you switch your concentration from the calf to the tendon. Because tendon rupture is a common malady of runners, I recommend a regular change in concentration to this area.

Hamstring Stretches. The next group will stretch the hamstring muscles. Since hamstrings are the primary driving muscles of running, they are the ones that can be overdeveloped in relation to flexibility and muscle balance. One of the best exercises for these muscles is the "hurdler's stretch." Simply place the back of the foot on a high resting spot such as the back of a chair and lean forward. Remember to keep the knee straight and increase your bend toward the leg very slowly and gradually. Just at the point of burning pain hold the position for ten counts and repeat several times.

Another good technique for stretching the back of the legs, as well as toning the upper torso, I call the "bungee cord stretch." This is especially good for individuals who insist on bending over and touching their toes because it "has always kept them flexible." However, touching your toes in this way can be damaging to the lower spine, which must support the weight of the upper body as it is being pulled to the earth by gravity.

In order to avoid this hazard, simply obtain a standard 3/8-inch length of bungee cord about twenty-five inches long. This can be purchased in any auto parts store. Now, hook one end of the cord on the top hinge of an open door between the door and the frame. With your back to the door hold the other end of the cord over your shoulder with both hands and attempt to touch your elbows to the ground. Be sure the hook is secure and everyone is clear just in case it should come off the hinge.

For those who don't mind spending a little money for a gadget that will help you gain flexibility and strength I might suggest the Apollo exerciser or Exer-Genie device. With this device attached to the top of a door, you can stretch the majority of the muscles while remaining upright without leaving your back exposed to the pull of gravity. It also can be attached at the bottom of a door for other strengthening and stretching exercises.

Proper stretching, however, need not require any equipment at all. For those who aren't addicted to the traditional toe touch and don't mind sitting on the floor to stretch, the same benefits can be achieved without the worry of back problems. Simply sit down on the floor with your legs outstretched, grasp the balls of the feet with your palms, lean forward, and hold for ten seconds at a point just before you feel pain. Doing this several times a day will rapidly increase your flexibility measurement.

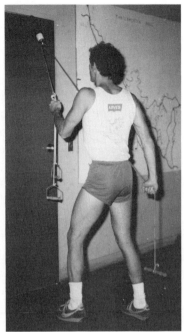

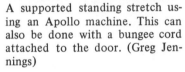

A supported standing stretch using an Apollo machine. This can
also be done with a bungee cord
attached to the door. (Greg Jennings)

Alternate arm pulls with an
Apollo machine. This exercise
develops the muscles used for
good posture and power in hill
running. (Greg Jennings)

Not only must we stretch the muscles, we must also strength-
en them. Since the primary driving muscles that are used in
running will be strengthened by running, strengthening exercises are necessary for those muscles that are occasionally
used but not necessarily developed during running. As the explanation for the basis of the SILK measurement reveals,
equalizing muscular strength in the entire body can both increase proficiency and prevent injury.

Some muscles of primary concern are the quadriceps muscles, located between the knee and the hip on the opposite
side of the hamstrings. Stronger quadriceps are necessary to
give balance to the developing hamstring muscles. They will
also help prevent shock to the knee, aid in hill running, and
assist you in mounting your horse. A good way to strengthen
them is to sit on a table with a weight suspended from your
foot. Straighten the leg, lock the knee, and hold for ten sec-

onds. Relax and continue for one minute on each leg. Riding a bicycle or an exercycle as often as possible will also strengthen the quadriceps.

Another muscle group that needs to be strengthened is the anterior tibialis, or shin muscles. To strengthen the shin, sit cross-legged in a chair and firmly grab the front of the foot with the hand opposite the foot being exercised. Now attempt to flex the foot in all directions while maintaining continual resistance against it with the hand. Do this for about one minute with each foot or until a slight burning pain occurs. This, in combination with your "foot fist" and running barefoot, should prevent any problems related to weak shins.

Two-man horizontal pull-up. (Greg Jennings)

Strength and Flexibility

"Strength and Flexibility Rating" (table 3) is based on five measurements: push-ups, bent-knee sit-ups, horizontal pull-ups, flexibility, and the backward run. The push-ups are the standard military push-up on toes and hands for men and knees and hands for women. A maximum two-second pause between repetitions is allowed.

The horizontal pull-ups test will measure the maximum number of nonstop pull-ups that can be completed. These can be performed by having another person stand over you while you are lying on your back on the floor. Reaching up and locking your hands with his and keeping your body straight, attempt to pull your chest up toward him as in a rowing motion. This can also be accomplished by placing a broomstick across two chairs so you can lie on the floor underneath it and raise yourself forty-five degrees off the floor in a similar manner.

Flexibility is measured by sitting on the floor with legs extended in front of you. Place a yardstick or tape measure between your legs so the "one-inch" mark is toward your

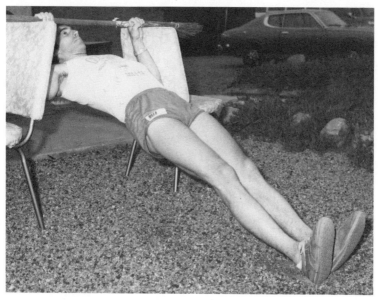

A horizontal pull-up using a supported broomstick instead of a partner. (Greg Jennings)

crotch and the fifteen-inch mark is on a line even with heels of your feet (not your shoes). With the tape in position and your heels about twelve inches apart, reach forward with both hands. Stretch as far as possible without bending the legs. and hold your fingertips over the number you can reach without bobbing, until a reading can be made. For example, reaching your heels would be a score of fifteen inches.

The bent-knee sit-ups must be accomplished with legs bent at forty-five degrees and nothing holding the feet down. Palms will be placed against the forehead with elbows pointing forward. When the elbows touch the legs, the sit-up is completed and you return to the original position with your shoulder blades touching the floor. Your score is based on the number accomplished in one minute.

The backward run score is based on the number of seconds required to run 220 yards backward. The run should be done on a track, preferably with someone spotting for you so you don't have to look over your shoulder.

Measuring hamstring and lower back flexibility with a ruler. This is also a very good exercise. (Greg Jennings)

The final component of the entire exercise session should be relaxation movements. Such movements allow body temperature to begin returning to normal sooner. These movements also help accommodate the return of blood from the large muscles back to the areas of normal circulation. The result is a more comfortable post-exercise feeling that will help you look forward to the next exercise session.

All the relaxation movements are performed while lying on the back with both knees bent and heels about fifteen inches from the buttocks. Eyes should be closed and movements should be slow and almost effortless. First slide one leg forward and bring it back to position. Repeat this for the other leg. Then let the head fall to one side, bring it back to center, and let it fall to the other side, once again returning it to center. Then raise the hand so that the elbow is resting on the ground and the forearm is balanced. Let it drop and do the same with the other hand. The final series of movements includes tightening and then relaxing every group of muscles from the feet to the face.

Thus the ideal exercise session should be comprised of five components: warm-up, target zone aerobic exercises, strengthening exercises, stretching, and relaxation movements. If you are doing an indoor session, you might try to divide the target zone portion among several exercise stations. This will help develop different muscle groups as well as make the work less boring. For example, do a few minutes on an exercycle, then move to a jump rope, then move to a bench, and back to the exercycle. Continue the rotation until the allotted time is up.

Other exercises are mentioned in Appendix I with reference to the SILK rating. These, in combination with those mentioned, should suffice for preventive maintenance. However, to maximize your Ride & Tie performance, you should do as many other strengthening exercises as you can. Such exercises should relate to a powerful arm swing for hill work, an untiring back for riding, and strength for getting on and off the horse. I have illustrated some good exercises, and with your imagination you should be able to come up with some more. One of the best ways to bring other muscles into play is through other sports, such as handball, skiing, and gymnastics.

TABLE 3
Strength and Flexibility Rating

Test	Measurement	Points
Push-ups	less than 10	0
"	10-14	1
"	15-19	2
"	20-29	3
"	30, or more	4
Horizontal Pull-ups	less than 7	0
"	7-9	1
"	10-14	2
"	15-21	3
"	22, or more	4
Backward Run	more than 75 sec.	0
"	70-75 sec.	2
"	66-69 sec.	3
"	58-65 sec.	5
"	57 sec. or less	6
Sit-ups	less than 13	0
"	13-14	1
"	15-19	2
"	20-23	3
"	24, or more	4
Flexibility	less than 14 inches	0
"	14 inches	2
"	15-16 inches	4
"	17-19 inches	5
"	20 inches, or more	6

Combined scores:
Push-ups _____
Pull-ups _____
Backward Run _____
Sit-ups _____
Flexibility _____
Total Points _____

Life-Style

The training exercises, charts, and tests may seem somewhat complicated, time-consuming, and burdensome. If they do, it may be because we do not fully appreciate the need for postural efficiency and muscular strength and flexibility.

There should be few adults who are not willing to spend an hour of their day exercising their bodies in a sage and meaningful manner. I cannot think of a life goal, no matter how academic, materialistic, or aesthetic, that would not benefit from a healthy, physically fit body.

If you really want to improve the quality of your life and health, you won't mind doing exercises or filling out charts in order to feel better, to enjoy doing more and, perhaps, to live a healthy life longer.

Ride & Tie, however, offers an opportunity that goes beyond the acquisition of health and longevity. As a game, it offers an alternative more rewarding than winning. It puts us in touch with our complete selves, and reminds us of what we once were and of what we are capable of becoming again. Preparing for a Ride & Tie helps balance our personalities and interests. It gives almost everyone, male or female, young or old, a substantial reason to become fit. Rather than merely adding health and years to your life, training for Ride & Tie will give *meaning* to your life. For this, most people seem willing to exercise.

Dave Woods, for example, a thirty-four-year-old disc jockey, entered a promotional event at a rodeo in which he competed with other disc jockeys in a 100-yard running race. Although it came as no surprise to him, being almost fifty pounds overweight at the time, that race "almost killed" him. But on the same day, Dave decided to begin training for the 1977 Levi's Ride & Tie. When I met him at that race, he was no longer an overweight disc jockey. Instead, I faced a formidable looking horse jockey who, less than a year before, thought a "trot was something you did just to get into a lope." It is speculation, but I believe that Dave's incentive to prepare for Ride & Tie participation was more than the mere realization that he was out of shape. I think that amidst the atmosphere of the rodeo and the exciting talk of the new game called Ride & Tie, he was taken by a more profound motivation. That same motivation may have caused Peter and Martha Klopfer to travel across the United States to enter their first Ride & Tie as a celebration of their twentieth wedding anniversary, or the father and son team from Holland, Adrian and Ed Vandenhoogen, to prepare for and enter a Ride & Tie having never before been on a horse. Similarly, Walt Stack, sixty-nine, and his Navy shipmate from forty years previous, Hugh Bryson, sixty-two, were reunited in their preparation for the Marin County Ride & Tie.

I would be amiss if I suggested that these individuals did not possess some special characteristic. Not everyone exhibits the sense of adventure, the level of determination, or the courage and desire it takes to make such a commitment. But it is my belief that most people do have all these characteristics, and in many cases they just need to be brought to the surface. People want an opportunity to develop their full potential, but not in a sport where success is measured by winning and losing, or where meaningful participation is limited by one's lack of natural athletic talent. In Ride & Tie such talent takes a second seat to preparation and desire. Not everyone will accept the Ride & Tie challenge. Though there may be plenty of horses and open land there may never be enough participants. But for every person who undertakes the challenge there will be more who will reap the rewards of preparation. The enthusiasm and dedication that project from a training Ride & Tie team is contagious. The training knowledge of this book when used effectively will become wisdom, and with wisdom comes teaching. If you experience the importance of stretching, for example, you can be sure you will fervently pass the information on to someone else.

One Ride & Tie contestant, Bill Fordell, claims his training influenced his entire neighborhood. The acquisition of his horse gave dozens of kids their first opportunity to ride. Many, who were at first afraid, gained confidence, skill, and responsibility under his supervision. Two other adults in the neighborhood borrowed a horse and began training in response to a friendly wager by Bill and his partner. Several others took up jogging and were continually seeking Bill's advice and encouragement. Before long most of the neighborhood had either started running, quit smoking, or had begun dieting. Some formed pit crews for the two teams and a friendly rivalry ensued. A chain reaction occurred in which many people benefited.

Our preventive maintenance considerations are a matter of life-style. The exercises are the means to an end, but the end becomes the means to a new beginning. The Ride & Tie game both concludes and initiates a way of life. With this in mind, we can continue our preventive maintenance discussion with other life-style considerations that will affect our ability to attain our full potential both as Ride & Tie competitors and as human beings. The first consideration has to do with that popular American addiction, smoking. I do not have to lecture the aspiring Ride & Tie participant on the hazards of smoking. The facts are abrupt. Any athlete would benefit from the absence of smoke, your own or the "second-hand smoke" from people around you. The nature of Ride & Tie deems it necessary to train in wild, open meadows, sandy deserts, mountains, and forests. These open spaces, usually free of smoke and city pollution, are the best training grounds for any serious athlete, regardless of sport.

Another life-style consideration that relates to Ride & Tie preparation has to do with psychological stress. I have known more than one individual whose desire to participate in the Ride & Tie experience was stifled by life's many pressures and frustrations. Usually such pressures are related to busy time schedules, monetary considerations, and too many hours at the office. Unfortunately, the psychological downfall attributed to such overloads should not force you to abandon your Ride & Tie preparation. It is, again, a matter of priorities.

A friend once succumbed to such priorities. We shared the same philosophy of self-determination and love of life. Fresh out of the service, we decided to pursue our dream of an extended sailboat voyage. The preparation including taking full-time jobs to handle the financial responsibilities of the trip. With the jobs, however, came promotions, a sense of security, and haunting ridicule that only a fool would risk all for a vagabond sailing trip. As a result, I sailed alone.

When I returned, however, my friend seemed a dejected soul. With the discovery of Ride & Tie his spirits soared. Here was another chance at life's exuberance, this time without sacrificing the security of the job. But as we bought a horse and began training, he was offered a promotion to an out-of-town office and a raise. He never did participate in the Ride & Tie. Within two years he became addicted to cigarettes, valium, and alcohol and spent most of his raise on a psychiatrist. Fortunately, this story has a happy ending. I have learned that he quit the job and joined a group now travelling across the country on bicycle.

Because of the amount of stress in everyday life, it is easy to succumb to pressure and forget your priorities and goals. But a game like Ride & Tie can be an important contribution to balancing out our lives. If you decide to attain the goal of the Ride & Tie, you must not allow yourself to give in to psychological stress. Eliminate that stress by becoming physically fit, and the challenge of the Ride & Tie will become easier, and more important.

For Further Reference:

Astrand, P. and Rodahl, K. *Textbook of Work Physiology.* New York: McGraw-Hill, 1970.

Behnke, Albert R. and Wilmore, Jack H. *Evaluation and Regulation of Body Build and Composition.* Englewood Cliffs, N.J.: Prentice-Hall, Inc., 1974.

Brozek, J. and Keys, A. "Relative Body Weight, Age, and Fitness." *Geriatrics* 8 (1953): 70.

Clarke, Harrison H. *Application of Measurement to Health and Physical Education.* Englewood Cliffs, N.J.: Prentice-Hall, Inc., 1976.

Ismail, A. H., Falls, H. B., and MacLeod, D. F. "Development of a Criterion for Physical Fitness Tests from Factor Analysis Results." *Journal of Applied Physiology* 20 (1965): 991.

Jacobs, Donald T. *Physical Fitness and the Fire Service.* Boston: National Fire Protection Association, 1976.

4

Cross-Country Running Techniques

One step at a time,
Each movement in rhyme,
With the earth, you're in close harmony.
Like the sea and the sand,
As it shifts with the land,
You run in the wild to stay free.

By now you are probably champing at the bit to commence your actual distance running. If you have reached your SILK rating and understand the previous life-style discussion, then you can don your running shoes and head for the hills. It is preferable, however, that you make the transition from your regular target zone exercise to running gradually. If you alternate your runs with cardiovascular exercises, such as rope skipping, bike riding, and bench stepping, your body will be able to adapt to running more easily. The transition should be complete after two weeks. Then you can save your original exercises for those rare days when it is impossible to run, or for augmenting your running program. Remember, however, that your stretching and strengthening exercising should continue indefinitely.

Hills and Distance

Although most runners and running coaches recommend that beginners save hill training until they are comfortable with long distances on the flats, this caution is not applicable for Ride & Tie training. In Ride & Tie we are not using hill training to develop strength and stamina for track or road competition. We are using it to train for hill competition. The rugged, hilly terrain of a Ride & Tie course may be found in few other distance races.

Waiting to tackle hills until you are comfortable with flat distance wastes many months of training. Changing to the hills would be like starting all over. Your flatland running technique would be of little help. I have seen beginning runners who trained for up to a year on roads and tracks become totally frustrated with their first attempt at hill running. But this is not to say that beginning with hill running will make training an easy chore. It was Shakespeare who said, "These high wild hills and rough uneven ways draw out our miles and make them wearisome...." Hills must be met with respect and deliberate concentration. Overexertion can occur rapidly, but by adhering to the following guidelines, hill running can be exhilarating.

It is helpful if you have hilly courses nearby, such as motocross trails, bridle paths, fire roads, and cow trails. Unless your horse is boarded at a place too inconvenient for everyday commuting, it is best to train on the same terrain on which you will be riding. If none of these courses are available for everyday running then you will have to find hilly roads. Roads at least provide you with an exact measurement of your mileage. The last resort is to find a single, steep hill that you can incorporate repeatedly into your run, even if it requires running numerous repetitions.

It is essential to run every day in training. Although significant improvements in running ability and fitness would occur with only four days per week, running every day promotes an internalized need for good daily workouts. After about five weeks of everyday running, your training will become a habit; this will make motivation easier. Eventually, a need for consistency will make your running a natural priority. Running every day will also prepare you for the combined schedule of running and horse training. The final three months of training require that the horse be ridden almost every day. If you and your partner are unaccustomed to setting aside time for daily training, it will be difficult to meet the needs of you and your horse. By running every day from the beginning of training, you will be better able to put in the extra time required to train and condition the horse.

The time spent on each day's run is also an important factor. As you have experienced, if you started training with our preliminary fitness stage, cardiovascular improvements can be made with only fifteen to twenty minutes of exercise at the target zone. However, as you also may have noticed, such a short time may not create the training routine you need. Each session will require much self-determination to get started, because the euphoric stage of exercise does not occur until after forty-five minutes of effort. This is when the body has adjusted to the various metabolic changes resulting from the extra work, and revitalization of the body cells is in full swing.

It should be remembered that we are no longer concerned with merely improving the cardiovascular fitness level. We are now concerned with running and riding a distance of thirty to forty rugged miles. Twenty minutes a day is not adequate preparation. Although you should eventually strive for a minimum total mileage of seventy-two miles per week, your minimum should be six miles or forty-five minutes a day, whichever comes first, or a total of thirty-six miles per week. In this way, you will achieve the maximum results with a minimum of stress. A workout less than forty-five minutes daily is not sufficient to reach the performance gains desired. Nor would a caloric expenditure of less than 600 calories per hour be sufficient.* With this in mind, you can use the Caloric Output chart in the following chapter to determine alternate activities that could substitute for an occasional run.

Obviously, the more mileage you can accumulate without stress or injury, the better. But running 100 or more miles a week, especially on hilly terrain, is unrealistic for most of us. After training for a number of Ride & Ties, you will be prepared for practice runs of 1/3 to 1/2 the distance of the race. Your body can usually perform adequately in a race two to three times the distance of your training sessions. For example, the beginning runner who runs eleven minutes per mile in order to maintain his target zone will have to run a minimum of just over four miles to meet his minimum daily requirement of forty-five minutes. However, to meet his minimum weekly mileage, he would have to make longer runs on other days.

*Ali Tooshi, "Effect of Three Different Durations of Endurance Training on Cholesterol, Body Composition, and Other Fitness Measures" (Ph.D. diss., University of Illinois, 1970).

He might do daily mileage of 4, 4, 8, 4, 4, 8, 4, . . . for a total of 36 weekly miles.

This type of schedule allows you variation and flexibility without sacrificing total mileage. Unless you are ill, you can always squeeze in forty-five minutes of running. If you are an advanced runner, this may not seem much time. But on those occasional days when you are fatigued or very busy, this is the minimum necessary to maintain consistency. Short, easy runs on such days will take the pressure off.

Running distance and frequency are important considerations for Ride & Tie preparation. More important, however, is the maximum intensity of each run. It should be emphasized that your heart rate increases rapidly when running up hills. You should monitor your heart rate carefully and continually to assure you do not exceed your limits. In fact, until you are running about fifty miles per week, it is preferable to stay as close to your lower limit as possible without going below it. Because of the close relationship between oxygen intake and heart rate, this will help assure that you are continually fueling your body with sufficient oxygen for a smooth but beneficial run.

If you are running at a pace that allows your muscles enough oxygen to avoid "borrowing" energy from other chemical sources, then you are running at a steady state or aerobically. At first the performance level at this rate may be low. But as training continues, your ability to take in and use more oxygen will improve your performance. If, however, you require oxygen in excess of your ability to supply it, then biochemical cycles will supply energy to the muscles temporarily until the oxygen debt forces you into a state of exhaustion. Working at a heart rate within the upper half of your target zone may cause you to work anaerobically, or beyond your ability to furnish sufficient oxygen to the muscles.

If you allow your body to become exhausted it will retaliate with defense mechanisms and warning symptoms, including insomnia, frequent illness, increase in pulse rate and blood pressure, lack of enthusiasm and energy, stomach disorders, lower back pain, and susceptibility to injury. An excellent way to determine if you have overtrained on a particular day is to note if the second-day run is affected by that of the previous day. Keeping a running diary can help, but the way you feel is a better guide. This will also help you determine when to increase your efforts.

Remember, the goal is endurance. By making sure the following requirements are being met, you should be able to run good distances. (These same considerations can be applied to your horse.)

1. Make sure you are running aerobically. Go slow enough so you are able to carry on a conversation.

2. Make sure you have trained enough to burn fat efficiently in your muscles. This will naturally occur with slow, steady muscular development through running, stretching, and light resistance exercising. The better developed the muscles are the more effective are the enzymes that metabolize fat.*

3. There must be enough glucose in the bloodstream at all times to supply glycogen to the brain. Premature exhaustion may thus be a result of dietary deficiency and the inefficient use of energy.

4. Make sure you remain adequately hydrated.

You should run at a steady pace slightly above your lower heart rate limit, keeping in mind your long distance goal. Competition requires too that your anaerobic capability is in tune. Ride & Tie competition often requires you to work beyond your steady state. You may have to make up for lost time if your horse is delayed in a Vet Check and you may sometimes be forced to cover more distance than your pace will accommodate. Often, a close race and a competitive spirit will force you beyond your aerobic capacity. Fighting against a nervous horse, or just trying to get on one, can call on anaerobic systems.

The mere excitement of the race often gives one an explosive surge of energy. One competitor relates a story in which he was starting up a steep grade after tying up his horse.

* Perhaps this is why Roger Bannister ran his first four-minute mile after having started his weight-lifting program. He had not been using weights when he was defeated in the 1952 Olympics. Similarly, one of the world's fastest runners, Ron Clarke, makes gymnastics, weight training, and stretching an integral part of his training. By increasing the quality of their overall musculature, runners are able to increase their ability to utilize fat as energy.

As he was rounding a narrow bend, he heard the pounding of hooves from behind. Because he was in no hurry to run up the hill, he stepped aside and watched the commotion. Five horses were in the group, but only three were mounted. The riderless horses were racing frantically ahead, and the riders seemed unable to keep up with them. The horses were five abreast on a road only wide enough for four. The riders were screaming both at their horses and at the other riders, trying to get running room. By the time the group passed the competitor, they were in a state of pure chaos. The horses' mouths were lathering with white foam, and one man's leg was accidentally pushing a rider out of her saddle. In a few seconds they disappeared around the corner. The runner was so excited by the whole affair that he nearly sprinted to the top of the hill, half-expecting to find a pile of broken bodies. He ran so hard, he says, that he had to walk down the other side of the hill just to recover.

Anaerobic capacity can also be a tactical asset in Ride & Tie. In the Marin County race I was running along a narrow path, covered on each side by thick manzanita and tick bushes. I had entered the trail less than one hundred yards ahead of a group of riders who had just mounted their horses. I knew if I continued running at my efficient steady state they would soon catch up with me, and I would be forced to crawl into the bush and wait for them to pass me. Rather than lose this valuable time, I chose to sprint to the end of the trail, where my horse presumably awaited me. I knew that I would be able to sustain a pace sufficient to stay in front of the horses, for the 300 or 400 yards to the end of the trail, because, in addition to aerobic training, I had also trained anaerobically.

Once you have attained a weekly running mileage of about fifty miles, training almost exclusively at a steady state, you can begin occasional overloads to develop anaerobic capacity. Gradual adaptation is just as important in developing anaerobic capacity as it is in developing aerobic capacity, flexibility, and muscle strength. An all-out run of seven miles or less should be made no more often than once every ten days. During your daily runs, all-out efforts should be made only three or four times, each for a maximum of two or three minutes. As you increase your ability and your weekly mileage, you can increase the anaerobic sessions according to the way you feel the next day. With the above exceptions, all distance running should be performed at a steady state. It is important in hill work to maintain a consistent effort, regardless of the slope. Thus, your speed over the ground will vary, but your effort will remain constant.

In order to reduce this self-imposed limit on speed without exceeding a steady state effort, you should, from the start, be conscious of hill-running techniques that employ the concept of mechanical efficiency. Mechanical efficiency refers to the ability to run with the lowest possible oxygen cost at a given speed, whether uphill, downhill, or on the flat. In other words, if two individuals, equal in degree of fitness and desire, were to race up a hill at the exact same speed, the one with the best mechanical efficiency would use the least energy and recover faster.

In order to attain the maximum mechanical efficiency during hill running, fundamental running techniques should be mastered. Because Ride & Tie is predominately a hill-running activity, appropriate techniques are described for easy reference. Uphill and downhill techniques have been treated separately because of their unique differences. If you con-

"Eyes on the trail in front of you" is the rule of thumb for running downhill at any time. (Scotty Ray Morris)

centrate too much on one aspect, you may disregard another. But with understanding and practice these techniques should serve you well.

Efficiency in Uphill Running

Motion. We have already talked about heart rate pacing on uphill runs. Overworking the heart will produce an oxygen deficiency, which will cause a buildup of lactic acid and slow you down. It is important, however, that heart rate pacing is based on continual movement. It is mechanically inefficient to stop completely when the heart begins to beat too rapidly, to wait until the rate slows, and then to continue. It is a matter of momentum: the forces required to set the body in motion from a still position require more energy than if the body is already moving. Thus, even if you must slow down considerably, your mechanical efficiency will still be higher than if you had stopped completely.

Velocity. Mechanical efficiency is also related to the rate of muscular work. We have already seen what happens when the rate of work is too fast, but slow movements can also be inefficient. For example, there is a point at which the steepness of a hill makes it more efficient to walk than to run. This occurs when the runner, in order to maintain a steady state, must run so slow that many of his actions are wasted in vertical movement instead of over-the-ground progress.

On such occasions, the muscular contractions involved in an *elephant walk* afford a more economical pace. By using the elephant walk, I have often kept up with competitors who were jogging up steep inclines using up almost twice the energy. The elephant walk is simply a striding hiking pace. In the military it is often referred to as a *route step*. The pace is vigorous. The use of somewhat different muscles requires practice. On slopes steeper than 40 percent (100 percent is equal to forty-five degrees) it is most efficient to push off each thigh with the wrist, while arms are rigid but slightly bent. (Be sure to push off the leg before the leg leaves the ground.) On slopes nearer to 25 percent, arms should swing rhythmically at the sides to help propel the body upward. These figures are, of course, approximate, and depend on your level of conditioning. To determine your efficiency level more precisely, you will have to experiment. If your rate of forward, uphill movement is approximately the same walking as it was when you were running at your maximal steady-state pace, then you will know when to walk. Since slopes will constantly vary, you will have to shift back and forth from elephant walk to run. In this way momentum can be maintained.

On hills with inclines greater than about 65 percent, maximizing efficiency becomes more complex. On such hills, the slow rate of static contraction with the elephant walk could reduce efficiency. However, if you run continually, you will eventually reach a point of inefficiency, if you run for a long time. But maximum mechanical efficiency can be obtained by lunging vigorously uphill as fast as possible until anaerobic buildup becomes obvious, and then doing the elephant walk until the oxygen debt is paid off. Then repeat the cycle.

The velocity of muscular contraction is closely related to mechanical efficiency in uphill running. The most important variable is the incline at each particular moment of effort. For beginning runners, however, the principle applies even on moderate or level terrain (see figure 1). It is also important to be aware of the various operations involved. Experiment until maximum efficiency is achieved, and then practice until it becomes natural.

Figure 1

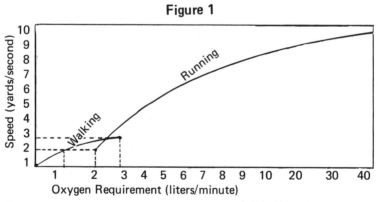

Source note: F. Henry, *Research Quarterly*, 24 (1953): 169.

Note: The diagram illustrates oxygen cost versus the linear speed of running and walking. It shows that mechanical efficiency varies with speed, an important concept in hill racing.

Posture. An incorrect uphill running posture will also decrease mechanical efficiency. As in all running, the spine should be as straight as possible. However, when running uphill the entire body should lean slightly forward. This posture should be shared by as much of the body as possible, from the head to the Achilles tendon, to minimize overbending the spine at any point. If you lift the knees high and keep your feet moving, this will also help minimize overbending.

It is also important to concentrate on *lifting* the torso. Lifting refers to actively using the upper body in the uphill effort. Without the lifting action, the upper body becomes deadweight. Lifting is also important in riding. As you are springing up the hill off the front of your feet, you should concentrate on lifting your upper body just before the legs' lifting action. Although the center of gravity should be kept low by tightening your back muscles and lowering your arms and shoulders, your chest should be wide and protruding for maximum lung expansion. To put the whole posture together, it helps to imagine guy wires attached to your head, the center of your chest, and the center of your pelvic girdle, all pulling you evenly and steadily up the hill.

Arm Swing. The most crucial aspect in lifting your upper body is arm swing. Your arms should swing parallel to your legs as you run uphill. The arc is made by the lower, outside portion of the elbow, and the upward stroke of the arms helps lift the body up the hill. The peak of the upward arm swing should occur at the same time as the pushoff of the same side leg. This will accomplish several things. First, by having the hand and arm at their peak at the moment of maximum uplift with the same side leg, the weight lifted by that leg will be less than if the arm were positioned closer to the axis of the body.

Second, the arm swing thrust will help carry the body forward. The faster, more powerful you desire your stride to be, the faster, more powerful the pumping action of your arms must be. It is important, however, that you make the change from the level run to the hill gradually, with little exaggerated arm movement at the base of the hill, and increase it as needed. When nearing the peak of the hill, begin reducing both stride and arm swing. Begin assuming a more upright posture so you are not leaning after you reach the peak. These actions will help keep you from overworking now that the end of the hill is in sight. It is important to reach the top in good form so you can run the level or downhill part that follows.

The third effect of such arm swing involves upper body lift and thrust. This effect relates to pulling the arm that is opposite the driving leg. Bringing this arm forcefully back will automatically augment the forward motion of the other arm. The backward movement of the hand should seldom go past the back of the thigh. It may be helpful to imagine that you are pulling yourself up the hill by a rope.

The pulling action can be experienced on level terrain during fast sprints. The faster you sprint, the fuller and more vigorous your arm swing. The difference is that in level running the arc of the arm swing is diagonal to the legs. Each hand will alternately cross a coordinate at the mid-center of the abdomen. This arm swing keeps the body running straight and reduces surface resistance to the air. In running, the forearms should be parallel to the ground and the hands gently cupped with the thumbs resting on forefingers. The backward pulling motion should incorporate a slight downward twist of the wrists.

The last benefit of arm swing in uphill running is that it provides the necessary rhythm to coordinate the rest of the running motion. The arm swing should keep the body in balance while it is struggling to conquer the hill.

Proper technique in arm swing is important and should be practiced until it becomes natural. The forearms should remain level with the ground, except at the top of the swing where the hands should be pointing slightly upward. Make your motion with as little exaggerated effort as possible. Your running will be more efficient if you keep your movements as limited as possible.

Foot Placement. Use natural footholds to allow for optimum spring and minimum inclination at impact, even on rough terrain, to increase mechanical efficiency. Where average steepness is consistent, the irregularities under the feet can vary as much as ten degrees. If the foot lands on one of these steep irregularities the muscular contraction necessary to lift off requires more energy than if it had landed only inches away on a flatter area.

A good Ride & Tie hill runner should not run straight up a hill. Careful observation and practiced reflex will allow you to choose the most efficient path without a lot of traversing. In some areas it may be necessary to plant the foot on a flat spot sideways to the hill. In such areas, a sideways push-off with the foot instead of a forward push-off will help you maintain your momentum without straining your foot. The sideways effort brings different muscles into action, and gives a temporary rest to the normal working muscles.

Psychological Factors. Efficient uphill running is a function of physiochemical, psychological, and volitional responses. These responses can cause increases in heart rate regardless of the physical demand of a particular task. Such increases are a result of experience and can be unlearned with proper training. You can increase your uphill running performance by acquainting yourself with these phenomena and developing techniques to overcome them. This will prevent you from being psyched out either by a hill or by a competitor. No doubt the image of a long, steep hill can intimidate you to the point of exhaustion. Tests have been administered to hypnotized subjects who exercised without full awareness of the work intensity. Results showed significantly lower oxygen uptake and heart rates than when participants did the same task without being hypnotized.* Often I have found myself running up a hill comfortably and steadily, staring at the ground. Looking up to see what is before me, I immediately have difficulty continuing up the hill, as it looms before me. If, however, I refocus my attention on the ground, I can continue my pace until I have reached the top, almost without knowing it.

There are several ways to develop the self-hypnotic ability to overcome the intimidation of a hill. One is simply not to look. Without the full awareness of the extent of the work ahead of you, you may be able to avoid intimidation. This technique, however, will not work for everyone. Some people will do better to look up at the hill and attack it defiantly.

*Robert W. Bullard, "Exercise Physiology," in *Physiology*, ed. Ewald E. Sekurt (Boston: Little, Brown & Co., 1971), p. 681.

However, it will take training to develop this successfully. I recommend never stopping, resting, or reducing your steady-state effort while you are ascending a hill. If it becomes essential to do so, the rest should be spent imagining that you have slowed down only because you have reached your horse. Then, while you are resting, pretend to be untying and cinching up the horse and preparing to mount. You can then continue your "rest" while pretending to be riding your horse up the hill at a slow pace. Although this process may appear strange-looking to a passerby, it will serve to develop an attitude about a hill that will keep you from being intimidated by it.

Not resting on hills, however, does not mean doing the entire training run without a rest. Such a restraint would detract from the joy and relaxation that running should provide. A rest somewhere along the trail can serve as a reward for getting to the top of a hill without stopping. Never stop immediately at the peak of a hill. Continue running until you have reached flat or downhill terrain, and your heart rate has returned to its lower limit.

Once you have mastered these uphill running techniques, you can employ them to psych out an equally conditioned competitor, who may not be as well trained in these techniques. On certain slopes, for example, you could gain on an opponent by alternating your pace between lunging and elephant walking. When you are within about ten feet of the competitor, try to remain behind so that you are not observed. Continue your elephant walk as long as you can maintain the same distance between you and the competitor. When you reach a point where you can reach the top or a turn at a faster pace without fatiguing, then it is time to make your move. Estimating this distance requires that you have trained well enough to know your limits and that you have mastered mechanical efficiency. Once you have reached the top and disappeared out of sight (at which time you resume steady-state work), you may have achieved a psychological advantage. You have made your opponent aware of the increased difficulty of catching you, thus increasing psychochemical fatigue, as well as destroying some of his confidence.

Chemical changes causing an increase in respiratory responses are not unusual in competitive events. Increased concentrations of *catecholamines* in the bloodstream resulting from excitement or psychological stress can significantly increase heart rate and deep breathing.*

Such increases are sometimes helpful in preparing the body for exertion, but in distance racing this type of pressure usually reduces efficiency. Reducing the importance of winning or losing is the best way to ease this pressure.

Efficiency in Downhill Running

Pacing. Safety and injury prevention should be a greater concern than downhill speed. Running downhill too fast often results in nasty falls, causing twisted ankles, injured knees, and back injuries. Running too fast downhill also places excessive friction between the foot and shoe, causing painful blisters. Such high speed can cause injuries, even when wearing insoles and several pairs of socks. Even-paced running is one of best ways to avoid such problems. The following techniques will give you the control necessary to assure you maximum downhill efficiency without excessive speed. However, if your momentum gets out of control, lean backward and make zigzagging turns until you are running at about ninety degrees to the hill. At this point you will be able to stop without excessive stress on the body and can begin running again at a slower, more controlled, pace. Trying to stop an out-of-control descent can be as bad as continuing the pace.

Posture. The posture in downhill running should be almost identical to normal running posture. Your body should be perpendicular to the slope, leaning neither forward nor backward. The abdominal muscles should be tight and the chest should not protrude as much as in uphill running. This will help you maintain a low center of gravity, while minimizing the jarring.

Concentration on the abdomen is very important in downhill running to prevent a frequent malady known as *stitches.* Stitches are sharp pains experienced in the side or abdominal

Catecholamines are chemicals released by the adrenals to prepare the body for "fight or flight."

region. Stretching of a weak diaphragm or a spasm caused by inefficient breathing will bring on stitches. They occur most often in downhill running because runners frequently lean too far back, putting a strain on the diaphragm.

Incorrect breathing causes the thoracic area to expand while the abdomen tightens, resulting in unnatural breathing. In order to breathe correctly, the abdomen should be relaxed during inhalation in order to allow the abdomen to expand. On exhalation, the muscles of the abdominal wall should be contracted. Without proper movement of the abdomen, breathing will be impaired, resulting in stitches. Proper movement and air exchange is called *belly breathing*. Belly breathing can be enhanced by exhaling while yelling or groaning, and strengthening the abdominal muscles.

Arm Swing. Arm swing is one of the most important aspects of downhill running control. Proper arm swing gives the downhill runner stability, balance, directional control, and rhythm. Arm swing should vary with your speed and the incline of the hill. As in level running, movements should be relaxed with little wasted motion, and forearms should be parallel to the ground.

On inclines from 5 to 50 percent, arm swing should increase in proportion to the increase in incline. The arm swing should increase with the slope until, at a grade of 50 percent, the hands move across the body at right angles. This sideways swinging motion will provide lateral stability without impairing rhythm. When making sharp turns at this speed, put extra force in the swing as arms move in the direction of the turn. By so doing, you will keep the weight of your body toward the inside turn, and avoid slipping to the outside.

When the slope increases beyond 50 percent, or if you want to increase your speed drastically, running rhythm becomes less important than balance. At this point the arms should have little swing, and should be held wider apart, as though you were balancing on a tightrope. In order to maintain rhythm control, however, you can rotate your arms in small circles, such that the outward motion coincides with the footstep on the same side.

On hills steeper than about a 75 percent grade, your running rhythm should be sacrificed totally. Your descent

Forceful lateral arm swing in the direction of the turn is necessary during a downhill run on a curve. (Greg Jennings)

should be uneven and interrupted. Arms should be spread wide and the hands held open rather than cupped. Going down this steep a hill is comparable to snow skiing on moguls (bumps on a ski slope). You should constantly change directions, slowing, changing pace, and evaluating your descent. Take advantage of loose shale and dirt if it is deep enough to dig your heels into and slide.

Foot Placement. Foot placement on the downhill run should be similar to that on level terrain, landing on the heel and coming off the toes. Exaggerating this motion can help control your pace. Extreme care should be taken that the feet do not land in chuckholes or on other irregularities in the terrain. Footholds should be used to avoid these areas. On such terrain, your run will zigzag and be irregular. Taking advantage of footholds on a rugged downhill run takes extreme concentration and dexterity. It also requires that the entire foot, lower leg muscles, and ligaments are well strengthened and stretched.

Eventually your feet will acquire "eyes" of their own, but downhill running always requires great concentration. The best way to watch for footing is to pick a point on the road or trail about fifteen feet in front of you and then run to it, scanning the area before you. On arriving at the point, scan ahead to another spot and repeat. This maneuver must be practiced, so don't run too fast until you can do it with control and concentration.

Base-of-Hill Technique. Another technique that will improve efficiency can be employed when approaching the end of a downhill run. By properly applying this technique, the changeover from downhill to uphill, or downhill to level, running can be made smoothly with maximum speed and minimum stress. Familiarity and practice with base-of-hill approach can help to keep you ahead of close competition.

This technique can be observed by giving an experienced trail horse his lead on a downhill run. The horse will maintain a controlled pace throughout the descent at a slow lope or steady trot. As the end of the hill comes into view, however, the horse will naturally break into a faster run to gain momentum for the next hill.

The same maneuver should be practiced by the runner. Throughout the downhill run, you have been concentrating on controlling your speed. You should maintain good balance and lateral stability; your downward gravitational force will increase steadily. For the following reasons, it may not be efficient to maintain this form and attempt to make the changeover after reaching the bottom: 1) the gravitational impact at the bottom of the hill can be stressful to your knees, hips, and spine; 2) a fair degree of effort will be required to change the style and force of locomotion necessary for the coming level or uphill run; and 3) you will not be taking advantage of an opportunity to use your downhill momentum.

You should begin increasing your pace about fifty feet from the bottom of the incline. Practice and experience will teach you how fast to make the pace. Your body should be relaxed at the start of the changeover to an uphill running posture, with the arms beginning to swing parallel to the legs. As you approach the last five to ten feet before the terrain levels off, your arms should pump vigorously, as though you were in a fast flatland sprint or were powering up a steep hill. Gravitational impact, therefore, is reduced by the uplifting action of your arm swing. As you hit the bottom, your knees should bend enough to absorb the shock of impact, and your abdominal muscles should tighten. If another uphill run is before you, this technique of using downhill momentum will put you up about forty feet before you realize it, similar to a roller coaster effect. If a level run awaits you, you should begin slowing gradually just as you lose the momentum of the downhill.

5
Nutrition

He laughed at the limping lad
Who failed to heed his feet.
But he cried to see the obese boy
Who knew not what to eat!

We must now prepare to tackle one of the most difficult life-style changes—our eating habits. It is also one of the most important changes in terms of preventive maintenance. I use the word *change* because in most cases this is what is necessary. More than 90 percent of all American adults have excess body fat. Millions of dollars worth of gimmicks, pills, fad diets, and figure salons have proven largely ineffective in solving the problem. In order to prepare for Ride & Tie, however, we must be able to deal with this problem.

Reduction of Body Fat

Reduction of body fat is basic to preventive maintenance. The additional weight is a burden on the musculoskeletal and cardiovascular systems of both you and your horse. (A horse can carry more live weight than deadweight.) This can be a dangerous burden on the unconditioned heart during the initial stages of training. The weight adds to fatigue and stress, and the addition of fat cells reduces circulatory system efficiency. Blood accumulates in fat cells, which, unlike muscle cells, do not pump the blood back. Excess fat also pulls the spine forward and may cause back pain. So, while you are stretching and strengthening your muscles, improving your cardiovascular efficiency, avoiding cigarette smoke, and maintaining psychological peace of mind, you must also lose your fat. This must happen before you begin distance training. But don't be frustrated. Once you become serious about Ride & Tie training, these tasks will become easier to accomplish.

77

The first step in losing body fat is to understand the development of fat: if you consume more calories than you burn you will gain fatty tissue. If you consume fewer calories than you burn you will lose fatty tissue. Given a few equations it is mathematically possible to determine and control weight loss or gain.

In order to help you with this portion of the solution keep a chart handy where you can calculate and monitor your level of fatty tissue. Record the caloric values of everything you eat in one column. (A *calorie* is the potential energy value of food.)* At the end of each day fill in columns marked "Output" and "Metabolic Constant." The "Output" column describes the average number of calories burned up in the day's activities. An estimate of caloric expenditures can be figured from the following chart, or you can find a more complete listing in a basic diet and nutrition book.**

Caloric Output (calories per hour)	
Desk work	60
Auto repair, janitorial work	120
Light carpentry	240
Digging ditches	420
Bowling	120
Golf, tennis doubles, walking 3.5 m.p.h.	240
Tennis singles, hand lawn mowing	360
Handball	600
Cycling at 13 m.p.h.	600
Stretching exercises (per minute)	3
Strengthening exercises (per minute)	7
Jogging at 5 m.p.h.	420
Horseback riding at trot and gallop	475
Running at 8-10 m.p.h. or on hilly terrain	720

The "Metabolic Constant" column lists the average expenditure of calories required to maintain your bodily functions such as digestion, heart action, and secretory activities of the

*Most bookstores sell pocketbooks listing the caloric value of foods. Or, an excellent book, *The Composition of Foods*, by B. K. Watt, and A. L. Merrill, can be obtained by sending $5.00 to *The Composition of Foods*, US Dept. of Agriculture, P.O. Box 17873, Tucson, AZ 85731.

**Adapted from *Exercise Testing and Training of Individuals with Heart Disease or at High Risk for its Development; A Handbook for Physicians*, The Committee on Exercise, American Heart Association.

glands. The adult basal metabolic rate is approximately 1.0 calorie per kilogram of body weight per hour for men and 0.9 calorie per kilogram per hour for women. (One kilogram equals 2.2 pounds.) This figure is only approximate as each individual's metabolism is different, but, it should be close enough for our purposes.

Once you have entered the day's input and output figures, subtract the difference between output and input and put the remainder in a "plus or minus" column. Input surplus should be preceded by a plus sign and output surplus by a minus sign. When the number of minus calories exceeds the number of plus calories by 3,500, you have lost one pound of fat, because one pound of fat contains approximately 3,500 calories.* You should not try to lose more than five pounds per month, nor should you sacrifice good nutrition to lose weight quickly. Once you are involved in the mechanics of calorie monitoring you will find yourself in much better control of the situation. The caloric output of your training exercises will not mean much in comparison to, say, a large piece of chocolate cake, but the exercises will help you control your eating habits by improved cellular nutrition. As muscle mass increases, enzyme characteristics will improve your body's fat metabolizing efficiency. These changes, however, will not produce instantaneous results. Changing dietary habits, even with exercise, is not physiologically or psychologically easy. You will have to work at it for two or three years before your dietary patterns become automatic. This should not alarm you because it will take the same amount of time to reach your peak as a distance runner and Ride & Tie competitor.

A beginning athlete should not attempt to progress any further until well underway with the training program. Once

---

*It is important to remember that the number of calories expended is more significant in preventing extra fat gain over a long period than the number expended in the short-term output. Regular aerobic exercises increase the quality of muscle enzymes so they metabolize fat more effectively. Anaerobic exercises, however, tend to burn more glucose than fat. By replacing intramuscular fat with muscle cells, body metabolism changes to such a degree that calorie-counting becomes less important. Thus, any diet that excludes exercise will not be effective in the long term.

you have attained the recommended SILK rating you will be ready to enter the more advanced stage of Ride & Tie preparation.

The science of nutrition is engulfed in controversy and myth. However, with enough exposure to many research conclusions, one can sift through until some common denominators are uncovered. Although regular exercise is the most important element, there is increasing evidence that certain dietary considerations are also important in attaining your optimal level of performance and health. The demands of Ride & Tie training and competition require that the body be in top physical condition.

Just as fat control is important in preventive maintenance, it is also important in considering efficiency. The body composition of a Ride & Tier should be lean in comparison to the average American, if he wants to perform optimally. In marathon runners it has been shown that maximal aerobic speed increased 5 percent for each 5 percent drop in body weight.* Improvement in the horse's capabilities in relation to reduction of the rider's weight is equally impressive.

The most important guideline in figuring your ideal weight is the way you feel during intense physical training. If you are keeping other factors constant, including gradual increases in distance, adequate SILK, and sufficient rest, then you can continue losing weight until you feel a loss of energy and strength. When this occurs, simply return to a slightly higher weight. When your strength and energy return you have found your ideal weight. Your goal then will be to steadily maintain this weight.

In some cases there will be no decrease in body weight at all, although there may still be a significant decrease in body fat. This is because, although fat takes up more space, muscle tissue weighs more. If you are "training on" muscle while you are taking off fat, you may not see the results on a scale. But you will see and feel the difference and know when you have attained your ideal form.

The crux of athletic nutrition is learning to listen to your body. Simply experiment with the variables until your body

*Editors, *Bike World* magazine, *Food for Fitness* (Mountain View, Calif.: World Publications, 1975), p. 63.

responds one way or the other. The problem, however, is in knowing enough fundamental variables to make the process of elimination viable. Body weight is one variable. A second variable, one which is much more complicated, is vitamin and mineral efficiency.

Vitamins and Minerals

Vitamins and minerals are organic compounds that occur in minute amounts in our foods and are essential for metabolic functions. Increases in metabolism resulting from endurance activities such as marathons and Ride & Tie may require amounts in excess of the recommended average. In order to give you some idea of how vitamins and minerals can rectify certain performance problems, I have listed some general guidelines below.* It should be emphasized, however, that although the chemistry of a vitamin is the same whether it comes from a bottle or from food, *I recommend that your vitamin modifications come from a selection of natural foods containing the desired vitamin.*

Self-diagnosis and treatment of vitamin deficiencies is a complex affair. For very serious problems, you should see a doctor, but in some cases improvements in efficiency can be achieved by self-diagnosis and treatment. Although we require a great deal more education regarding body chemistry interpretation, we should realize that our health is based on efficient use of vitamins and minerals.

Dr. George Williams, of the Institute of Health Research in San Francisco, agrees. He has started a program where an individual receives a complete health profile based on his or her hematology and blood chemistry. With this profile comes an explanation of each element. The blood tests are taken once a week for a five-week period to assure an accurate average. If the tests are taken twice a year they can be compared to determine if any changes or deficiencies have taken place. Only by comparison can such a determination be made because each individual's blood chemistry is unique.

*Adapted from C. H. Robinson, *Normal and Therapeutic Nutrition* (New York: Macmillan and Co.); and Mildred Jackson, *The Handbook of Alternatives to Chemical Medicine* (Oakland: Lawton, Teague Publications, 1975). *The Composition of Foods* also lists the vitamin and mineral content of foods.

Vitamins and Minerals

Calcium	relates to reaction time, muscular contractions, and bone solidity
Copper	necessary for formation of iron and hemoglobin
Phosphorus	relates to absorption of glucose from the intestine for energy
Magnesium	relates to prevention of muscle cramps and nervous irritability
Iron	relates to prevention of anemia and reduced red cell count
Cobalt	relates to the synthesis of vitamin B_{12} and appetite regulation
Zinc	relates to functioning of the heart
Vitamin A	maintains visual acuity
Vitamin B_1	involved in carbohydrate metabolism; relates to improvements in appetite, mental depression, and constipation; helps stop muscle cramping
Vitamin B_3	helps reduce excessive tiredness
Vitamin B_6	relates to protein metabolism; may improve nervous irritability, weakness, and abdominal pain; helps prevent stiffness of joints
Vitamin B_{12}	relates to formation of red blood cells and improves anemic responses
Vitamin C	relates to absorption of iron; possible antiviral agent
Vitamin D	regulates absorption of calcium
Vitamin E	may lengthen cell life; reduces oxidation of vitamin A
Vitamin K	responsible for blood clotting ability
Vitamin P	helps dissipate body waste

It is important to determine what we *should* put into our bodies for maximum performance, but it is also important to know what *not* to put in. This brings us to the controversial issues pertaining to processed foods, food additives, and vegetarianism. In these areas man's behavior and physiology again may parallel the horse. The horse, if allowed to indulge in unlimited amounts of concentrated, premixed rations will often eat itself literally to death. There is medical evidence to indicate that man may be no different.

The widespread use of processed foods in the United States has been scientifically linked directly or indirectly to such diseases as coronary heart disease, cancer of the colon and rectum, appendicitis, hemorrhoids, diverticulosis, gallstones, phlebitis, and obesity. The major portion of our "refined diet" has been stripped of vitamins, minerals, trace elements, fiber, and other nutrients. It is no wonder that the life span in our country ranks eighteenth in comparison to other nations. White flour is a good example. When wheat is milled into white flour, up to 80 percent of the essential nutrients are lost. Vitamin E is destroyed altogether and less than 5 percent of the dietary fiber remains. Even when flour mills were required to begin "enriching" the flours because of serious outbreaks of pellagra and beriberi, only the chemical elements directly related to these diseases were replaced. Thus, of the twenty-two nutrients that were taken away during milling, only four were returned with enrichment.

Food manufacturers have also added thousands of chemicals that may be detrimental to our health if consumed too regularly. These excess additives may impair the body's ability to function efficiently. Perhaps the most damaging substance in the American diet is sugar—including refined table sugar, brown sugar, corn syrup, honey, and molasses. An explanation of its effect may motivate you to adjust your eating habits. If you decide to restrict your sugar intake, do it gradually. It may not be necessary to eliminate sugar totally from your diet, especially if you exercise regularly, but the total amount of sugar currently consumed by the average American is horrifying.

Simple sugar gets into the bloodstream too quickly and in too great a concentration. This is especially true of refined sugar, from which trace elements that help metabolize the sugar have been removed. When the sugar enters the bloodstream, insulin is secreted in an attempt to regulate the now-too-high blood glucose level. Because of the abnormal increase in the glucose level, the amount of insulin is also too much, and results in a deficiency of blood glucose. During the depression that follows, more sugar is usually ingested and the cycle repeats itself until organs and metabolic functions are damaged. Such dysfunctioning can lead to health problems ranging from chronic depression to chronic coronary artery disease. It also inhibits the proper metabolism of fat, which is essential for running long distances. The list of what too much sugar can do is frightening. Sugar:

- increases the viscosity of the blood
- increases the transit time of wastes
- increases gastric acidity
- increases urinary and oral acidity
- increases triglycerides and cholesterol
- impairs phagocytosis (the ability of white blood cells to collect bacteria)

If we are to remain healthy and perform at our best we must become aware of what is happening and adjust our eating habits based on the conclusions of our research. Until technology develops indigestible additives to preserve our foods, and controls are placed on toxic chemicals in our foods, we should attempt to at least reduce our intake of these chemicals. I recommend you acquire Douris and Timon's *Dictionary Of Health And Nutrition*, which describes the majority of additives and their degree of safety.*

General Diet

The subject of athletic nutrition and diet inevitably leads to a discussion of vegetarianism. For this reason, in spite of the controversy, I feel compelled to offer some basic knowledge about vegetarianism so perhaps you can reach a rewarding conclusion.

It should be remembered that mankind has a tremendous ability to adapt. As a result of our migrating and conquering history we have spread ourselves into all kinds of environments. As a result of barren environments and climatic changes we learned to eat other animals in order to survive. With the invention of weaponry our power over the animals gave us a convenient source of food. The slaughterhouse in-

*Larry Douris and Mark Timon, *Dictionary of Health and Nutrition* (Moonachie, N.J.: Pyramid Publishers, Inc., 1976).

creased the convenience until fashion, habit, and protein education made meat a permanent fixture in our diet. Thus, man has become a meat-eater. But, if structure governs function, then meat-eating may be an unnatural overindulgence that needs to be reevaluated. Our body structure bears closest resemblance to that of the ape, whose diet is vegetarian.

There are, however, good endurance runners and Ride & Tie winners who eat meat during training. And, there are many societies, including the Eskimo, that thrive on meat. But these facts represent mankind's ability to adapt. In measuring maximum performance, however, they should be weighed against the fact that many top marathon runners eat little, if any, meat. You should be willing to put it to the test. If you eat a wide variety of raw fruits, vegetables, and whole grain products, enjoy an occasional steak or hamburger. (Hopefully it is pasture-fed and therefore not subject to the many additives injected in feedlot cattle.) But watch your performance and see what happens if you cut down on meat.

Until several years ago, when I began researching the field of physical fitness, I was an avid meat-eater. As I read and learned more about fitness, I began what I call the "wild man's diet." With this diet I avoid foods that would be considered rarities if I were living in an abundant forest. I allow myself fish and abalone only if I have caught it myself, eat honey only occasionally, and try to eat a wide variety of raw vegetables. As a result, I feel stronger and healthier than ever before.

This worked well for me, but listen to your body, watch your performance, and experiment with a variety of diets to find the one that works best for you.

A diet, advocated by Nathan Pritikin, calls for a drastic reduction in all types of fats, sugars, and refined products and an increase in complex carbohydrates. This diet, combined with vigorous activity, could prevent and possibly reverse heart disease. The decreased fat in the bloodstream enhances the transfer of oxygen. At the same time it reduces the potential source of atherosclerotic plaque that forms scars along the vessel walls. Although exercise seems to be the most significant physiological cause of reducing atherosclerosis, results achieved with a good diet seem to confirm that it may significantly contribute to reducing the possibility of acquiring one of the nation's foremost killers—heart disease.

If your regular diet is optimal, then there is no need to make many "special" changes when preparing for a big race.

Our consumption of oxygen is of primary concern. Without the developed ability to take in and utilize oxygen we will not be able to take advantage of any other form of energy. The more oxygen consumed, the more energy is available, but if you train enough to acquire an adequate oxygen intake ability, you will want to maximize the energy capabilities of your pre-event food intake. The following information should help clarify the confusing ideas about pre-event eating.

If you are a meat-eater, you should not eat meat for at least three days prior to the big event. Your body requires up to 30 percent more energy to digest this protein in comparison to the requirements for carbohydrates. Only about 92 percent of the protein is hydrolyzed and absorbed into the bloodstream as compared to 98 percent of carbohydrates. The three-day figure is used because that is usually how long the digestion process can take depending on your metabolism. Maximum efficiency will not come from a pregame meal of concentrated protein. (Note: your body will receive enough protein for metabolic functions by complex carbohydrates during this period.)

Since carbohydrates are the cleanest burning fuel at 98 percent (fat is about 92 percent), this is the type of food on which we will focus our attention. Carbohydrate energy comes from its end-product, glucose. Glucose becomes available for immediate energy in the bloodstream. It is stored as glycogen in the liver and muscles, and some is stored in adipose tissue after being synthesized into fat.

During the event the glucose available for energy is used up quickly, probably within ten or twenty minutes depending on your blood level at the start. About 100 grams of glycogen can be stored in the liver to replace the depleted glucose in the bloodstream. Even when glycogen stores begin to deplete, you can utilize the 200 to 250 grams available within the muscles. This glucose energy is available for the muscles only and cannot regulate the blood sugar level. Through carbohydrate-loading this level of glycogen can be maximized.

Carbohydrate-Loading

Carbohydrate-loading is a process whereby the primary muscles used during the event are depleted of their glycogen stores to make them ready for a large refilling. This occurs by exhaustive running on a moderate carbohydrate intake four or five days prior to the event. This depletion will stimulate the glycogen-storing enzyme to fill the working muscles to the brim during the high carbohydrate intake of the next three or four days. This period of high carbohydrate intake need not be extreme because you should have ceased the exhaustive workouts of the depletion stage.

The problem with this whole affair is that the maximum glycogen storage capabilities of the liver and the muscles, even if completely used up, could only furnish 1,200-1,600 calories. According to exercise manuals, four hours of riding and running would require more than 2,400 calories. Our solution lies with the third glucose storage depot, the adipose tissue.

Adipose tissue is found in subcutaneous tissue around the organs in the abdominal cavity and is laced throughout the muscle tissue. The glucose not otherwise utilized is synthesized into fat and stored in these areas. When this source of energy is called upon as a last resort, there is a bonus. One gram of this fat energy is equal to nine calories when oxidized as opposed to the four calories relinquished by one gram of carbohydrate. This use of energy explains how some people have survived up to forty days without food. There also is evidence to indicate that the body can be "trained" to make the changeover to fat oxidation more efficiently. This entails a continual high-quality diet with frequent workouts that call for an excess of 1,600 calories. With such muscular activity, mitochondrial enzymes increase their capabilities to burn fat as energy.

Now, many carbohydrate-loading advocates frown on the use of fats for energy because of the drop in performance intensity. There is truth in this because oxidation of fats will occur faster than the body can take care of the waste products when carbohydrates are restricted. Such incomplete burning of fuel leads to anaerobic muscle contractions and a buildup of lactic acid that eventually reduces the amount of work that can be performed. However, by introducing small quantities of carbohydrates or glucose into the bloodstream during the oxidation of fats, such waste products can be limited. The trick is to train at long enough distances at a slow enough rate so as to condition your body to oxidize fats while keeping a reserve of blood and muscle glucose. Otherwise, if too much intensity of effort is required in a race, the glucose will be used in preference to the fat until it is used up and none is left to "spark" the fat metabolism.

Therefore, it is my conclusion that the principles of carbohydrate-loading be applied on a more or less permanent basis, to be fairly consistent throughout yearlong training. Continuous cycles of high, complex carbohydrate intake with regular exhaustive workouts using *long slow distance,* will prepare the body to operate optimally at all times.* This way temporary adjustments can be avoided. You should do two or three exhaustive workouts—"exhaustive" in terms of maximum distance, not maximum effort—per week. During the process, vitamin, mineral, and protein needs should be sufficient if a wide variety of complex carbohydrates are consumed, and if the majority of foods are uncooked and whole. Daily intake can be determined by monitoring running performance, weight, and quality of bowel movements. Food should not be eaten within six to twelve hours of your maximum effort training run or race. I recommend the following sample dietary procedure (assume race time is 9:00 A.M. Saturday):

Thursday morning	plain yogurt with honey, raisins, and bananas; or a large variety of citrus fruits; or a bowl of rolled oats with prunes
Mid-morning	herb tea, fruit juice
Lunch	cook vegetables and boiled potatoes (sprinkle with brewers yeast and wheat germ)
Dinner	very small portion of fish, eggs, or low-fat cheese with cooked vegetables (Drink only liquids until bedtime.)

*Long slow distance (LSD) is a training method popularized by *Runner's World* consulting editor, Joe Henderson. It involves long-distance workouts at a slow, steady pace, rather than race pace. The pace, according to Henderson, allows the runner to go longer and enjoy the psychological, as well as the physiological, benefits of running.

Friday morning	grape juice, toast (no butter), and a banana
Lunch	spinach spaghetti with tomato sauce
Dinner	liquid meal only (use commercial products that use soya powder as a base instead of milk, or a mixed vegetable juice)
Saturday morning	warm glass of water with a little lemon juice
Race time	half-pint of electrolyte drink five minutes before start

During this forty-eight-hour period drink as much water as possible, chew your food well, and exercise moderately. Avoid roughage, fats, nuts, raw vegetables, milk, meat, and simple sugar. (Note: I recommend not having a solid meal during the thirty-six hours preceding race time.) The goal is to modify your training and your dietary cycle to approach a maximal effort run at your peak level. With practice, you will know when this is.

Food consumption during the event is also important. Since it takes the stomach from four to six hours to empty solid food into the intestinal tract where the absorption of nutrients takes place, solid foods are out. The ingestion of fluids is important because, next to oxygen, water is our most valuable nutrient. It becomes extremely important in a Ride & Tie because of the large amount of fluid lost through perspiration.

Fluid Replacement

During the race, we simply need to drink a fluid that contains small quantities of glucose to combine the need for fluids and small amounts of carbohydrate or glucose to help prevent the incomplete oxidation of fat energy. It may be that glucose gives us a "brain boost" to alleviate fatigue caused by the central nervous system's response to low blood sugar. Increasing blood sugar may simply reduce this built-in warning system. The amount of glucose in the drink should be less than 3 percent in order to allow the fluid to leave the stomach and enter the bloodstream as soon as possible. (The more sugar, the longer it remains in the stomach.) Accordingly it will take about fifteen to thirty minutes for the liquid to leave the stomach and become effective. It should be consumed near the start because urine production ceases after about twenty minutes of running. Therefore, the plan should be to have a drink (about ½ pint) every fifteen to thirty minutes starting at the beginning of the run.

We should make the most of our liquid by adding an important group of ingredients—*electrolytes*. The liquid we lose from our bodies, especially during hot and prolonged exertion, is not pure water. It contains a crucial balance of substances essential for transmitting nerve impulses necessary for the contraction of muscle fibers. These substances, called electrolytes, include numerous elements of which the most important are potassium, magnesium, and sodium. Of the three, it is most important to replace potassium and magnesium during competition because greater percentages of these elements are lost through perspiration. The exception to this is when an individual's diet is low in natural foods containing sodium or if he has not acclimatized adequately to heat during training.

In fact, ingestion of too much sodium during exertion may be more of a threat than too little sodium. An increase in extracellular sodium causes a withdrawal of fluid from the cell, which can upset crucial osmotic pressure and fluid balances. Also, the body is better prepared to handle a sodium deficit than it is to handle the rapid removal of potassium and magnesium from the circulation.

The loss that can occur with potassium and magnesium, however, can be more inhibiting. When the body begins depleting these electrolytes, the synthesis of substances necessary for muscle contraction becomes impaired and muscle cramping, nausea, and dizziness can result. It is essential to include these electrolytes in our race liquid. There are several commercially manufactured drinks available that include the proper amounts of electrolytes and a small amount of glucose. These drinks include ERG, Body Punch, "ade" drinks, and several other brands. Check with fellow athletes for their recommendations, or make your own by diluting orange or tomato juice. But make sure you are getting the right balance because glucose, amino acids, and fatty acids all depend on the correct concentrations of electrolytes. It is important to remember, however, that the complex workings of our bodies depend on the interrelationship of many nutrients. A deficiency of any single substance can prevent the proper reactions and create havoc in the entire system. In addition, water is constantly necessary for regulating body temperature, carrying nutrients, and lubricating the joints.

Whatever effort we put into "listening" to our bodies, learning about its processes, measuring its capacities, and analyzing its chemistry will be rewarded with health and vitality.

Part Three
The Horse and Rider

6
The Rider

In times now gone past
Men rode far and fast,
Hitching their dreams to a star.
And now we recall
The thrill of it all.
All hail the return of the centaur!

Changing your concentration from running to riding is a natural transition that will take little effort if you understand the similarities between each sport. Runners are already familiar with the fundamentals of balance, muscle coordination, timing, strength, and body control—the same fundamentals used in riding. These similarities involve realizing that both human and horse are naturally suited long-distance running animals. One is reminded of the Tarahumara Indians, who are able to run a deer to exhaustion. Reflections of these similarities should be applied to planning conditioning programs for yourself and the horse.

The prerequisite for this transition, however, is an understanding of the horse and the basics of riding. Without this understanding it will be difficult to overcome any fear and mistrust you have about the horse. You will not learn to ride well until you have mastered this fear. It may take some time to find the ideal competition horse, but the basics of riding can be learned on any horse. The beginning rider should take every opportunity to ride, so for this reason, I have preceded the chapter on choosing and training the horse with a chapter on general riding information.

Tack

When learning to ride, it is important to use the correct *tack.** This will make the riding experience more enjoyable and efficient for both you and the horse. Eventually, in rid-

* *Tack* is stable gear, especially articles used on saddle horses.

ing long distances, proper tack can prevent injury and soreness to the horse.

The first decision to be made concerns the type of saddle
to use. I recommend beginning with an expertly fit *English
saddle*. After you have learned to ride, you can experiment with
specially made endurance saddles. Individual preference based
on comfort and comparative observations of your horse's performance under various saddles, will help you pick the right
saddle. However, because English saddles put you in closer
contact with the forward movements of the horse, they are
the best for a beginning rider.*

You must consider the unique characteristics of the horse
wearing it in making your final decision. Ideally, the saddle
should be custom-made for the horse. Where this is not
feasible, you must use your own judgment. Fit, however,
should be your main concern. The saddle should fit firmly
against the horse's back. The front arch should clear the top
of the spine above the withers by about three fingers when
someone is seated in the saddle. If it is too low it will put too
much pressure on the spine, and if too high, the sides of the
withers and top of the shoulder will be bruised after long
rides. In this regard, it is easier to fit the horse with a *western
saddle*. In either case, see if you can try the saddle out before
making any firm commitments.

Although your own comfort is important, you should not
be too greatly influenced by the extra comfort of the heavy,
western saddle. On a long ride the extra width often causes
more discomfort than the English saddle. The extra weight
also can be detrimental to the horse's performance. Another
disadvantage of a western saddle is the standard *latigo* for
tightening the girth and the stirrup leathers, which are more
cumbersome to adjust than those on English saddles.** The
quick buckling girth strap used on English saddles will enable
you to quickly loosen the cinch at the tie-up to give your
horse more breathing room. Your teammate can quickly

---

*An *English saddle* is designed to set the rider's weight over the top of
the forelegs. A *western saddle* sets the rider's weight closer back behind the horse's center of balance. An English saddle is easier on a
running horse.

**Latigo* is a long strap on the saddletree used to fasten and tighten the
cinch.

cinch up before mounting. The quick-adjust stirrups are handy if both of you require different lengths. If you decide to use a western saddle it should be light and well built. It should also be a *forward design* saddle on which the stirrup leathers hang forward of center so that your legs will hang forward of the girth. The idea is that your seat on the horse should be as near the *withers* as possible because it is at this point that the horse is the strongest.* Many western saddles are designed for cow and rodeo work in which turning, stopping, and backing are more important than continual forward motion. Such saddles do not give you as good a forward seat as English or forward design endurance saddles.

One advantage of the western saddle is that with it, a horse can be ridden with a looser girth than normally required to hold an English saddle in place. And a slightly looser girth is of great benefit to the endurance horse. A moderately loose girth allows the horse more breathing room with less effort. However, I believe that a loose girth can be used as easily with an English saddle as with a western one. Being able to ride well without a tight girth (and without allowing the saddle to rub back and forth on the horse) has more to do with your riding ability and balance than the type of saddle used. A well-fitting English saddle can be ridden with a loose cinch if a *breast collar* is used and your balance is good.** The breast collar is a mandatory piece of equipment for the Ride & Tie horse, whether or not you ride with a loose cinch. It is attached to the saddle and the girth of the saddle to keep it from slipping too far backward on steep hills encountered in Ride & Tie. Personal preference and your horse's conformation will determine which type of breast collar to choose. As with the girth, the strap should be wide enough to avoid chafing of the skin. I recommend sewing sheepskin around the leather breast collars and using cinch covers on the girth strap.

If you are riding with a loose saddle, or your horse is low-withered, and you expect some very steep downhills on a particular course, you may want to consider using a *crupper*

---

*The *withers* are the ridges between the shoulder bones of the horse.

**A *breast collar* is a harness strap extending across the horse's chest in place of a collar around the neck.

Sheepskin makes an excellent saddle covering. (Scotty Ray Morris)

strap to keep the saddle from slipping forward.* Since some horses do not like a strap secured to their tails, you should give them a chance to get used to it. If the horse has a severe dislike for a crupper then disregard using it. It will require a fairly steep incline and a very loose girth before the saddle goes too far forward. In such instances it is usually preferable to dismount and lead your horse downhill on foot.

A saddle pad is a must, and should be thick enough to help spread the saddle weight evenly without forcing it out of shape. The best pads are made of thick, double-pile acrylic fiber that will not slip or crease. (A washing when it is new will prevent slipping.) A western saddle should be used with both a western saddle pad of acrylic fiber or matted hair and a folded wool blanket. With either saddle the padding should be tucked up into the saddle fork to prevent stretching the pad over the withers and allowing for ventilation under the saddle. The saddle pad should be kept clean to avoid bumps and rubbing that can cause infection.

Another piece of tack that you may or may not need is a running martingale. This device prevents the horse from pulling his head too high. A horse with this habit is more likely

---

* A *crupper strap* is a leather loop that passes under the horse's tail and buckles to the saddle. It offers protection to this sensitive area.

This Arabian, wearing only a halter, is free to eat and relax at a tie. (Scotty Ray Morris)

to stumble on the rugged, rock-strewn trails than a horse that carries his head properly. The martingale can be used either during a race or for teaching the horse to correct the habit.

A halter with an attached lead rope is essential for Ride & Tie. A horse should never be tied with the bridle reins, as the strength of a horse can easily break them. A horse attempting to pull away from a tie could injure himself since the reins are attached to the bit. Some horses have even managed to pull their heads out of bridles.

The halter should be nylon, with wide straps that buckle on the side. Make sure you buy the right size so that it is neither too loose nor too tight. The lead rope should be a half-inch in diameter and long enough to reach the top of the horse's tail. It should have a good snap, on both ends, large enough to fit around the diameter of the rope. The snaps should be good quality, so you can snap and unsnap them easily with one hand. With such a rig you simply pass the rope around a tree or post and snap the end onto the bridle to secure your horse. Another ring tied in the middle of the rope will allow you to tie around a larger tree. On a very large tree or when you are reaching back behind a bush, you can simply snap it back on the rope.

Some Ride & Tiers prefer having a plain-ended rope for old-fashioned tying. The advantage of tying, is that you can tie the horse the exact distance from the tree or post that you desire, regardless of the size. You do not want to tie the horse so long that he will step over the rope and trip himself or block the path of another horse and rider. Either possibility could be catastrophic. Although I recommend using snaps, every Ride & Tier should know how to make a regular tie in case a snap becomes damaged. Whether you use a clove hitch, a horse knot, a cow hitch, or a quick release bowline, the tie should be secure and easy to untie.

The bridle, in Ride & Tie, is a necessary evil to be used only on unpredictable or hard to control horses or by a rider lacking sufficient confidence and skill. I recommend, therefore, that all riders begin Ride & Tie training with a bridle, but eventually train to ride without it. Riding a horse without a bridle gives the Ride & Tie horse several advantages. First, the horse is able to move more naturally without the constricting pain and aggravation of a steel bit in his mouth. Properly ridden, he will be less susceptible to stress and nervous fatigue. He will be able to breathe and move his head freely. Secondly, using only a halter and lead rope will make tying the horse more efficient because there are no reins to slip over the horse's head and trip him and you will not waste extra time tying the rope.

Another reason the halter alone is more effective is because it allows the horse to graze unimpeded while he is tied. Without the bit in his mouth it is much easier for the horse to nibble at grass and leaves. This is important because if he is eating, he is relaxing, and less likely to notice stampeding humans and horses rushing past him. As a result, he will gain sufficient rest by the time he is needed again. Finally, riding with just a halter seems to produce better harmony between the horse and rider. Without dependency on the immediate control of the bit, the rider must be constantly aware of every change in the attitude and stride of the horse. If a group of horses are approaching from the rear, you must be able to feel the apprehension of your horse and respond with relaxation, confidence, and control before the horse reacts in fear or excitement. Riding in such close harmony with the horse will allow you to maximize the efficiency of the horse's energy output, capabilities, and intelligence. Knowing that you cannot rely on the control of a bit forces you to be a better rider. But, riding without a bit can be risky unless you understand your horse and are assured of your ability to control him. While you are learning to ride and attempting to train your horse to work without a bridle, you should use a bridle with a smooth, thick bit to avoid cutting the inside of the horse's mouth. The bit should fit snugly into the mouth just enough to cause a slight "smile." The leather should be adjusted accordingly, and should be well oiled to prevent chafing. If you choose, you may want to try a *hackamore*. Rather than a steel bit, a hackamore has a heavy noseband that pressures the horse into slowing or stopping.

Proper maintenance of riding tack is very important. Longer life of leather materials depends on keeping them clean and well oiled. You also should check the stitching and the attachments at the stirrups and the girth regularly and keep them in good repair. Riding with equipment in poor condition can cause real problems. Walt Schafer found himself in such a predicament. Eight miles after the start of the Olema Ride & Tie he was descending a winding trail 1,000 feet down to the Pacific Ocean on his horse, Flying C Kenya. As they came around a sharp bend, the right stirrup strap suddenly ripped apart at the stitching. Fortunately, Walt suffered only a minor groin pull and half a mile further he had a mounted pit crew member who was able to exchange straps with him.

Riding Apparel

As in choosing tack, chafing and soreness are important considerations when choosing riding apparel. Riding a horse over thirty-odd miles of rugged terrain can be extremely damaging to a naked pair of legs. Remember that you will be riding the same chaparral country that prompted the American cowboy to don heavy leather chaps. Sweaty horsehide, saddle leather, and narrow double straps from English stirrup leathers that pinch your calf are a few other things to consider when choosing clothing. In light of these factors, no normal equestrian would ever consider riding in skimpy running shorts. On the other hand, who would run hills in ninety-degree heat wearing blue jeans and riding boots?

The Ride & Tie competitor has attempted to solve this problem with several alternatives. One is to wear long baseball stockings, held up by elastic knee supports. The supports give additional padding to the portion of the leg receiving the most chafe. Or the stockings can be held up with garter belts attached to your running shorts. Another remedy that has worked effectively for some is homemade bloomers. They should be made of a light, porous material with elastic pant bottoms and waist. Those who wear bloomers say they keep them cool, dry, and protected, and are not a hindrance in running. I personally can't vouch for them as I haven't gotten up enough nerve to wear them yet. When the pain and agony of chafed legs strikes, however, there is little concern over how one looks. Pantyhose is also often recommended. Just prior to the Olema Ride & Tie, six-time women's division champion Dawn Damas, recommended, to a man whose legs were already somewhat chafed, that he wear a pair of pantyhose for the race. The man laughed. After the race, he approached her with raw, bleeding legs and inquired, "What kind of pantyhose?"*

Others, who prefer to run with as little clothing as possible, have experimented with saddle covering instead. That is best done by sewing a woolly piece of sheepskin around the surface of the saddle so it extends down and over the stirrup leathers. Be sure it doesn't slip or interfere with adjusting the stirrup and girth buckles. Be careful you don't develop a heat rash from posting on the wool. If these alternatives fail to meet with your approval and you are unable to invent your own means of protection, you just have to grin and bear it. It is a little reassuring to know that as you practice riding, your legs will become more accustomed to avoiding the pinching and rubbing that occur more often at the beginning of your riding career. Whatever clothing you wear should be light and unrestrictive so that sweat evaporation can take place. Cooling your body and preventing heat

*According to Damas, Sheer Energy by Leggs is the only brand, of the many brands she has tried in her several years of competition, that meets the demands of Ride & Tie.

Comfort, loose fit, and lightweight material are essential clothing in Ride & Tie. These homemade bloomers are perfect. (Mark Chester)

exhaustion should be the primary consideration when choosing riding and running apparel. Terry-cloth hats are helpful because they provide shade and can be soaked to keep your head cool. If plenty of water is available on the course, wear a shirt that will allow for maximum evaporation and drink lots of water. But if water is limited, wear a heavier shirt that will allow your body to maintain moisture longer. Also, don't forget suntan lotion for skin protection.

One final suggestion regarding your attire is to stash a pair of plastic bags near stream and creek crossings you will have to navigate during a race. These can be placed during a preride, and will prevent your shoes and socks from getting wet and heavy.

Grooming the Horse

After you have chosen the appropriate tack for your horse, it is important to carefully scrutinize your horse for possible sore spots both before and after a ride. Sore spots can occur for a variety of reasons, from improper riding to being unaccustomed to a new saddle. Riding an injured horse without remedying the cause is like running with a bad blister without taking care of it. The best time to make this survey of the horse is while you are grooming him.

Grooming the horse should be done both before and after a ride. Grooming removes waste products, prevents skin diseases, and stimulates circulation, in addition to allowing you to check for problem areas. Preride grooming will assure there are no skin wrinkles or debris to irritate the horse during the ride. Regular grooming also gentles the horse and accustoms him to being handled. It should be done with both a brush and a *curry comb* and only when the horse is cool and dry.* After a long ride, the horse should be walked down before he is groomed.

An important part of preride grooming is checking and cleaning the hooves. Be sure the shoes are not loose or overly worn and that all rocks and debris are removed with a hoof pick. To pick up a horse's front legs, run your hand gently down the back of the leg until you reach the *fetlock*.** Grasping the tendons just above the fetlock, lift while pressing against the horse's shoulder, thus forcing his weight on the opposite leg. To lift the hind leg, face the rear and gently stroke the back of the leg from the quarters to the *cannon*, using the outside hand.*** Pushing his weight onto the opposite leg with your inside hand or shoulder, lift the foot toward you so the leg is bent at the hock. Move it toward the rear until the horse is standing comfortably.

The Art of Riding

Once the horse is properly equipped, you can deal with the fundamentals of horsemanship. If you are learning how to ride or haven't ridden a horse for a long while, don't try to make up for lost time by initially riding too long. Regardless of your conditioning, your body must get adjusted to sitting in a saddle for any length of time. If soreness occurs, you can

*A *curry comb* is a comb with metallic teeth or serrated ridges, and is used to dress a horse's coat.

** The *fetlock* is a projection on the back of the horse's leg above the hoof. Fetlock also refers to the piece of hair on this projection.

***The *cannon* is part of the horse's leg, higher than the fetlock.

be assured that the problem will disappear as your riding continues. It is difficult to speak of getting saddle sore without thinking of a story told by Ride & Tie participant Walt Stack. Walt competed in the rugged 1977 Levi's Ride & Tie at the age of sixty-nine. A hod carrier by profession, Walt is an avid runner, averaging over eighteen miles a day. However, before he began training for the Ride & Tie he hadn't been on a horse in more than forty years. Responding energetically to the challenge, he plunged headlong into riding with an eighteen-mile ride. Later, after successfully completing the Ride & Tie, Walt was standing amidst a group of young ladies telling about his eighteen-mile ride that first day of training. He explained how he figured his first ride should be at least as long as his daily run. After all, the horse had four legs. He found, however, that it wasn't the horse he should have been concerned about. "My ass was sore as hell." He spoke frankly with his construction work lingo as he gesticulated with a bottle of beer in each hand. He described a dream he had that first night. Projected on his closed eyelids was a cartoon drawing of a large horse. The horse was standing on its hind legs, beating Stack over the buttocks with a baseball bat and exclaiming, "You silly S.O.B., this will teach you a lesson or two!"

The precaution is obvious. Overtraining can be as much a problem in riding as it is in running. Not only are you more likely to get injured, but a tired rider causes a horse to move poorly; thus the horse is more likely to be injured. Since the horse picks up on almost every vibration the rider transmits, it is important to relax while riding. The ability to relax while on the horse may be the single most important component of skillful horsemanship. In horseback riding, the ability to relax comes with confidence. Admittedly, it may be difficult to be confident your first time on an unfamiliar, one-thousand-pound animal. If so, you must instantly become a great actor. The horse has an incredible ability to perceive your apprehensions but he can be fooled. If you are not able to hide it completely, the horse will also become fearful and apprehensive. A fearful horse becomes tense and difficult to control. Even his involuntary, instinctual reactions can be controlled to some extent by a confident rider.

WALT STACK'S DREAM

Mounting

Mounting the horse is the first step in conveying this confidence. The horse should know what you are doing and be confident that it will be painless. Talk to him reassuringly without overdoing it, or he will suspect something is wrong. When you make your move, it should be smooth, fast, and effortless. You should land in the saddle lightly and reward him with a soft pat on the neck.

There are several ways you can mount a horse in Ride & Tie competition. Each has its advantages and disadvantages. The first is facing forward in the direction of his head. To do this, grasp the reins along with a hunk of mane with your left hand and take hold of the back of the saddle with your right hand. Springing off your right foot and pulling yourself up with the mane, set yourself comfortably in the saddle, moving your right arm out of the way of your right leg as it swings over. You can use the reins to restrain the horse if he is moving forward, but don't pull hard enough to make him move backward. The advantage of mounting this way is that you can observe the reactions of the horse more carefully by watching his head and eyes. This also keeps him pointed in the right direction. The disadvantage is that if the horse starts moving forward rapidly, you may experience difficulty mounting, especially after an exhausting run.

The second mount, however, allows you to swing into the saddle as the horse moves forward. With this mount you face the rear of the horse and turn the stirrup toward you. Grasping the mane and saddle as in a forward mount, you position your left foot in the stirrup, hop off with your right foot, and swing your right leg over the saddle. The disadvantage of this mount is you can't see in the direction the horse is looking and will not be forewarned of a possible distraction. Also, there is a tendency for the horse to turn around until it is facing the wrong direction. On narrow trails this can be dangerous.

Another effective mount for Ride & Tie is a running mount. I have found this both a time and energy saver, although it requires training and agility to accomplish correctly. It allows you to get your horse moving in the right direction from the start. This is important because the combination of a nervous horse, a tired runner, and a crowded path can cause problems. In many cases, a running start, hop, and jump will put you in the saddle with less effort than a more traditional mount. To accomplish this mount, start down the trail with the horse at a fast pace alongside you. With your right hand, get a good hold on the front edge of the saddle. With your left hand, grasp the mane and reins and continue running until you are able to hop up in rhythm with the horse's gait. Once you get the hang of it, the momentum will pull you right into place. Mastering this mount will take some practice because you must not land too hard in the saddle or the horse will learn to balk or sidestep attempts to mount. Another disadvantage of this mount is that you will have to find your stirrups while running. This can be difficult when the stirrups are swinging back and forth. The running mount is worth trying if you are riding with a very loose girth because it is easier to land your weight over the center of the saddle. Centered weight is a must when riding with a loose girth. It also should be noted that it is not always necessary to mount from the left side. A good Ride & Tie horse should become accustomed to your mounting from both sides. I have even used rear vaults effectively if the end of the tie rope was snapped to the halter so the horse could be untied from a mounted position.

Once you are seated comfortably in the saddle, you should pay close attention to your posture and balance. You should be relaxed, carrying your body without stiffness. The balls of your feet should be planted lightly but firmly in the stirrups with your toes slightly higher than your heels. (The length of the stirrup leather should be such that, with your legs hanging loose over the saddle, the stirrup should reach your ankle.) As long as you have equal pressure on both stirrups, you will always be exactly centered on top of the horse. Maintaining this balance can be practiced by riding with the loose girth style I have recommended. This way, you will have to keep equal pressure on each foot or the saddle will start to slip to one side or the other. In fact, you should learn to ride well enough that you can ride a horse through its gaits without using a girth and never allow the saddle to slip.

Balance, sitting light in the saddle and leaning forward afford proper forward momentum in riding. Proper posture is essential for endurance riding. (Scotty Ray Morris)

Another way to find the appropriate point of balance is to stand up in the stirrups. When you are able to maintain your balance without gripping with your legs or holding on with your hands, sit down slowly, keeping your legs in the same position. You are now balanced with your knee and toe in line and your heel, hips, shoulders, and head in another line. This position should sound familiar, because it is the exact toe off posture you should have when running. The only difference is that in running, the lines will form on the side on which the foot is planted. In riding, both feet are planted simultaneously. There should be a conscious forward impulse coming from the pelvic area and the hands in order to start the horse moving. The reins should be held delicately, but firmly. Your hands should be pointed in the direction of the horse's head so the communication transfer is direct and your energy focus is aimed in the direction of travel. A slight shift of weight, from the waist up, in the forward direction and a moderate amount of leg pressure against the horse's side will start you on your way. As soon as the desired pace has been attained, resume your natural upright position and release the pressure with your legs.

In order to slow or stop the horse, tighten your abdominal muscles and lean back slightly, attempting to make yourself heavier without tensing your legs. At the same time, gently pull back on the reins. When the horse has slowed to the desired pace or has come to a halt, immediately return to the more comfortable posture and release the backward pressure on the reins. The release of all pressures and the assumption of the relaxed posture is sufficient reward for the horse to obey your signals. It is important to apply these pressures only when you desire a change of pace or direction. Continually pulling and slacking the reins will confuse the horse just as using leg pressure to hold on will make the signal ineffective in stopping the horse. Gravity and forward momentum will carry you along when you are properly balanced so there is no need to grip with your legs unless you are riding bareback. Your body should be in perfect harmony with the horse's stride to maintain a constant pace. If he starts to increase the pace, don't pull back unless it is absolutely necessary. Instead, simply maintain the original position of your hands without relinquishing an inch to the pull of his head. The horse will usually respond to the restraint by returning to the original tension.

Turning

The same riding consistency applies to turning the horse. Turning pressures should be avoided until you want to change direction. When riding on rough, winding trails as in Ride & Tie training, it is best to use both hands to guide the horse whether it has been trained to mouth or neck rein. To make a left turn, lead the left side reins in the direction of the turn, pulling the horse's head gently to the left. At the same time, draw the right side of the reins across his neck and in the direction of the turn while applying slight pressure across the sides with your right leg. The horse will have a tendency to move away from the side where the pressure is applied. When the turn is completed, resume your normal position. Reverse the procedure for a right turn.

If you are riding at speeds faster than a slow trot on a winding trail, the horse should make the turns on the correct "lead." If you are making a left turn while in a lope (or canter) and the horse is leading with the right leg, he is more apt to stumble. This is because the leading leg is the only front leg that hits the ground while the other legs are in the air. If the horse is leaning into a turn without the support of the inside leg, he is off-balance. Normally, the horse will choose the correct lead naturally. If you notice he is on the wrong lead, slow him down to a trot. Then put him back into the canter while applying pressure with the outside leg and shifting your weight slightly over the inside shoulder. This should put him on the correct lead. To see if he is on the correct lead, look down and see what leg is coming forward on the third beat of the three-beat rhythm, the natural rhythm for this gait. It is interesting to note that most horses prefer the left lead because, like most people, they are usually "right-handed" or right-sided. They begin the power portion of the run with the back right leg which causes the gait to end its third beat with the left front leg. To demonstrate this, start out running and notice which leg it is that initiates the drive and which leg leads. Very often, while running, you will want to change your lead to relieve a leg pain or to change the work load. The same principle should be applied to the horse. By changing the lead, the concentration of effort is redistributed and fatigue and injury are less likely.

You also should note the similarity between forward propulsion in running and riding. Balance, gravity forces, consciousness of pelvic impulsion (as though a rope were pulling you forward), wrist and elbow position, use of hands, and overall body posture are almost identical in both riding and running. In order to really benefit from the comparison, imagine doing one activity when actually doing the other. If you are riding, imagine you are running instead of the horse. If you are running, imagine you are riding.

As Ride & Tiers, we need not be too concerned with the more formal and technical aspects of the various gaits. However, knowing how to trot is essential because it is the gait you are most likely to use over much of the course. It is also important to learn first because it is the most difficult gait to master. The trot is a two-beat gait in which the horse lands first on the left front and right rear legs and then on the right front and left rear legs, depending on which side is leading first. There is more vertical action with this pace so it is more difficult for the rider to maintain a comfortable and balanced seat. Remaining in the saddle during a trot can be uncomfortable and damaging both to the horse and the rider. The rider must learn to rise and lower himself in turn with the rhythm of the horse's vertical movement. This is called *posting*. The idea is to rise just as one diagonal is coming off the ground by pushing the thighs off against the saddle and standing slightly in the stirrups. Your buttocks should be slightly ahead of the saddle on the uplift and resting lightly on the saddle as the horse comes down. It will not take long to determine whether or not you are posting correctly. If you are, it will feel smooth and the horse will pace himself evenly. You will not tire as rapidly as if you were doing it wrong. You also will avoid tiring the horse if you are posting consistently so you are coming down as the horse is breathing out. If your rhythm is inconsistent, the horse's breathing will become irregular. It is also a good idea to change leads occasionally, so the horse doesn't tire on one side. This is done by sitting down for two beats and posting on the opposite lead.

If you are on a flat, even trail, you should increase the rate of your post until the horse catches up to you. This way you can obtain maximum speed without breaking into a lope. However, on rock or uneven terrain try to avoid the steady, posting rhythm and allow the horse to vary his rhythm and his stride. This requires more concentration.

Anticipation

There is one area in learning to ride where it is difficult to draw the analogy between riding and running. It is in what I call the "anticipation factor." The anticipation factor is important in terms of safety. The horse, unlike the runner, does not have the capability to analyze new and different stimuli and reacts instinctively with fear. For example, riding past a fence post on which a shirt is hanging and waving in the wind, could startle a horse into a sudden change of pace, a quick lunge to the side, or a sudden stop. Such an occurrence could cause the horse to fall over an embankment or jump into a barbed-wire fence. An unprepared rider could be thrown, or reacting in fear to the horse's unexpected movements, might find himself out of control on a runaway animal. The way to avoid such a calamity is to always be prepared for the unexpected. A good horseback rider anticipates any potential distractions to the horse. Although you allow the horse as much freedom of movement as possible, you must remember that you are "driving" him and the speed and direction are *your* choice, not his. It is up to you to recognize things that might startle the horse. Many problems can be rectified in training, but it is impossible to expose your horse to all the unexpected influences that he will encounter on a trail. When you see a potential problem, avoid it if possible. If it is not possible, slow the horse down, reassure him, and pass the obstacle without showing too much concern over it.

The best way to avoid horseback riding accidents is to anticipate potential hazards. Anticipating problems often requires a thorough understanding of your horse's capabilities in handling various types of terrains and environments. On occasion, however, it will be impossible to foresee something that will cause the horse to shy. A rattlesnake you cannot see, a silver coin shining in a creek, an animal jumping out in front of you, or an old metallic trail marker are all examples of things that could cause an unexpected reaction from your horse. When such things occur, your own reaction and sense of balance must come to the fore. Then, in addition to trying to avoid a fall, you must also be able to convey confidence and relaxation to the horse. He will trust your senses and overcome his fear if you convince him there is nothing to worry about. It is this communication that is the most challenging, exciting, and rewarding aspect of horseback riding.

This preparation will eliminate the majority of riding accidents. However, during the course of your Ride & Tie preparation, especially while you are just learning to ride, a stumble or a sudden movement may catch you unprepared. If you do get thrown or fall from a horse, the chances are most likely that your main concern will be the safety of the horse. You will probably wind up with a scratch or two and some bruises, but it is more than likely that your pride will hurt worse than your body. Such minimum injuries from a riding fall, however, are largely dependent on your level of SILK and your natural or learned ability to take a fall. Books on horsemanship rarely concern themselves with the prospect of falling from a horse. This is unfortunate in view of the increasing popularity of horseback riding and the occasional incapacitating injuries that might have been prevented through instruction. Athletes should be instructed in how to fall. Research indicates that the majority of severely disabling injuries suffered from falls, including severe sprains, broken bones, or head injuries, happened to individuals who had no previous athletic experience or who were in relatively poor physical condition. Nor have these individuals been instructed in how to fall. Research also indicates that the frequency and severity of rodeo injuries have decreased significantly since rodeo cowboys have started training and conditioning as athletes.

Athletic conditioning, in this sense, refers to the development of flexibility, strength, and cardiovascular fitness beyond that attained from horseback riding and rodeo events. The students in how-to-fall classes should be directed in calisthenics, tumbling, rope-skipping, and weight-loss programs. A saddled barrel suspended above sawdust can be used to develop balance and simulate falls from a horse. A judo expert should instruct the classes in correct falling techniques. This should not worry the beginning rider. It will simply reemphasize the relationship between preventive maintenance and participation in the demanding Ride & Tie. The development of your full potential in any endeavor cannot be done haphazardly. The more possibilities you can prepare for, the greater your chances for survival.

7
The Horse

With love and care
You can go far
Aboard your trusty steed.
Just give him food,
Good shoes and such—
The same things that you need.

Choosing your four-legged teammate for Ride & Tie can be an exciting venture. Depending on your particular circumstances and preferences, there are several alternatives to consider in obtaining a horse. One alternative, if you have the time and patience, is to raise and train your own horse from a foal. If you are going to invest this much time and energy in a horse (a horse must be five years of age before it can compete in a Ride & Tie or other endurance race), you should, however, be sure it meets the physical requirements for an endurance horse or that it comes from proven endurance stock.

Choosing the Horse

If raising a horse from a foal isn't realistic for you, you can consider purchasing a mature horse. If riding trails are convenient, owning your own horse can bring you many hours of pleasure whether or not you compete regularly in trail rides or races. If owning a horse requires you to board it and ride it several hours away from your home, you might want to consider a partnership to share the responsibilities and assure that the horse is ridden often enough. Ideally, of course, the partner should be your Ride & Tie partner. In fact, Ride & Tie can be looked upon as an opportunity to get involved with horseback riding at half the cost. Even when you both go "riding" at the same time (Ride & Tie style) or take turns riding and running together at the same pace, it makes for an enjoyable day.

The third alternative for obtaining a competition horse is to borrow one. Occasionally you will be able to find someone who would like to see the horse put into top condition for him. In fact, this is how my teammate and I got our horse for the 1977 Levi's Ride & Tie. My partner, a blacksmith, asked one of his customers if we might be allowed to try his purebred Arabian to see if he would be suitable for the race. The horse had been the family pet for eleven years and was not often ridden. We convinced the owner the horse would be happier in good condition, so he graciously turned him over to us. We named the horse "Potter," after the occupation of his owner, and shared the cost of his upkeep. When his owner saw the change in Potter's looks, spirit, and manageability after only a few months, he was very pleased. When the horse finished its first competition in fifth place against a field of the world's best endurance horses, he was ecstatic!

Some Ride & Tie participants borrow horses that will be trained and cared for by the owners themselves. These horses are usually proven endurance horses and the owners are usually endurance riders who aren't competitive enough as runners to make a good showing in a Ride & Tie. They "lease" the horse out to a team of good runners and riders. Prize money is usually divided evenly and a good finish in a Ride & Tie will increase the value of the horse. There are two advantages to such an arrangement. First, it allows you the use of a proven horse without the cost and responsibility of ownership. Secondly, it gives you more time to devote to your own conditioning. If a team still practices often with the horse, the results can be very positive. Not owning and training your own horse also has some negative aspects. For example, you may not learn to know the horse well enough to handle him well or to prevent some unforeseen circumstances. Or, you might not know the horse well enough to be able to work him at maximum efficiency. And, you simply may not experience the pride and satisfaction of training your own horse or the emotional bonding that occurs with the trials and tribulations of caring for your own horse.

Regardless of what alternative you choose, the prospective Ride & Tie horse should meet certain criteria. To begin with, a full or part Arabian is the best, although others will suffice.

THE HORSE AND HIS REGIONS

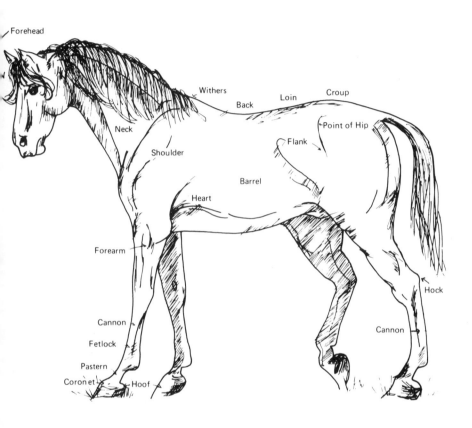

This drawing illustrates some of the parts of the horse mentioned throughout the chapter. A Ride & Tie horse, in addition to being from good quality, proven endurance stock, should have a strong back and well muscled legs.

Many types of horses have done well in endurance racing and Ride & Tie, but, on the average, none have done as well as horses with Arabian ancestry. In most of the top endurance races in the world, the highest percentage of finishers in the top ten are Arabians. From tests used to choose horses for the U.S. cavalry in the early 1900s, it was found that "the Arabian possesses more endurance and weight carrying ability, and a record for lower feed consumption, with freedom from unsoundness, than any other breed."* It should be remembered that not all Arabians possess the characteristics that will make them ideal endurance horses, and there are horses other than Arabians that possess such characteristics. The need, more importantly, is to become familiar with what characteristics make a good endurance horse.

The first consideration should be the animal's age. It must be a minimum of five years old before it will be allowed to compete, but a more mature horse usually is better suited to the rigors of endurance training. Properly cared for, a horse can continue to perform well up until about fifteen years of age. Of course, the younger you purchase the horse, the more years of riding he will afford you. It should be noted that Arabians mature a little later than most horses and seem to reach their prime around age eight. The second and most important consideration is the horse's conformation. As in humans, any imbalance in structure will be brought into play and magnified as mileage training increases. Although many imbalances can be somewhat rectified with corrective shoeing, you will be better off to avoid a horse that needs corrective shoeing. Poor conformation can cause incapacitating and costly injuries to the horse and prevent him from completing a successful Ride & Tie.

Generally speaking, the horse should look proper and balanced overall. The body parts should be joined together smoothly and nothing should seem out of proportion to the rest of the body. He should have a broad forehead with large eyes set well apart (long considered a sign of intelligence by horse traders). Large nostrils will allow him to breathe adequately. The neck should be arched and well muscled without appearing too short or too long. The shoulders

*Dancia Bacciocco, "What Breed for Endurance?" *Saddle Action,* September 1976, p. 46.

should be sloped about forty-five degrees to the ground to assure a full, even stride. His chest should be deep and wide for ample lung capacity and his withers should be prominent (at least as high as the top of his *croup*) in order to hold the saddle in place.* The ideal endurance horse does not have to be tall if he is well built. Almost any size person could do well with a horse about fifteen hands (one hand is equal to four inches). The horse should be compact, having a short, straight back. (This trait is inherent in the Arabian because it has one less vertebrae than other breeds.) Ideally, there should be no more than three fingers width between the last rib and the point of the hip. A horse with a long back usually will have too weak a loin area to cope with the rugged, hilly terrain.

The most important conformation considerations have to do with the legs of the horse. The quarters and forearms should be muscular. The cannon bones should be short and broad, and the knees should be large and flat, making the horse less susceptible to splints and fractures. Tendons should be thick and well defined. The legs should be straight, with hocks bisecting perpendicular to the rump and the knees standing straight under the shoulders. The illustrations should help you identify leg abnormalities in horses you will want to avoid choosing for endurance work.

If your eye is not experienced enough to pick up all the considerations of conformation, you may be able to determine related problems by watching the horse move through its gaits and by riding it through its gaits. If the horse overreaches, forges, or stumbles, it is a sign of poor conformation. The stride should seem even and smooth at both the trot and the canter (lope). He should move with an even rhythm and his rear feet should move along the same line as the front feet. As with the human runner, the heel of the horse's foot should land slightly before the toe.

There are also other important factors to look for when shopping for a horse. If the horse's skin is tight and he has a shiny coat, it is a good indication that he has been cared for properly. His hooves should be deep and wide with a good arch in the sole. His teeth should be evenly worn, an indication that he chews his food properly. A foul odor in his mouth could indicate gum infection. In order that you don't

*The *croup* is part of the horse above the hindquarter—the rump.

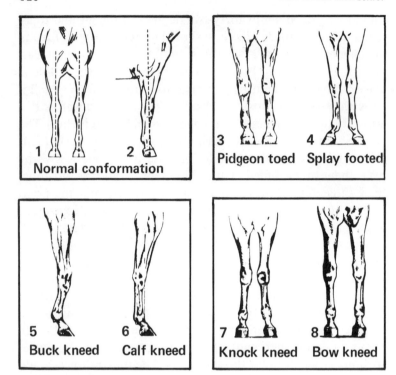

1 2 Normal conformation

3 Pidgeon toed 4 Splay footed

5 Buck kneed 6 Calf kneed

7 Knock kneed 8 Bow kneed

*Reprinted with permission from *Saddle Action* magazine.

discount an otherwise good prospect, it should be kept in mind that some of these inadequacies, such as overweight, dry hooves, dull coat, and uneven teeth, can be rectified with proper care. Similarly, certain bad habits, such as not allowing you to lift his feet, not trailering easily, or shying when you handle him, can be corrected. Before you buy an unkempt horse, however, be sure to have a veterinarian give him a thorough examination, including blood and urine tests, to determine any other health problems. In fact, it is a good idea to have a vet look at a prospective horse if you are not convinced of the horse's potential and suitability.

Disposition or spirit is one important trait that is difficult to change in a horse. In her book *Endurance Riding*, Ann Hyland includes this characteristic as one of the three major factors in choosing an endurance horse. She states, "Choosing the ideal horse means searching for one that combines good conformation, strong striding gaits and a generous but sensible temperament."* The horse should not be overly nervous. Such a horse will not pay attention to what he is doing on a rugged trail, and can get both of you into trouble. He also will waste too much energy. On the other hand, the horse should be very willing. The best way to determine if a horse possesses this willingness is to ride the horse up a steep hill. If he seems willing to continue without hesitation and tries even though he is obviously tiring, then you can be fairly sure he will be suitable for Ride & Tie, all other things being adequate.

One final suggestion that may be of help in obtaining a worthy horse is to look for horses registered with the Endurance Horse Registry of America. Although this registry is fairly new, founded in 1974, it is growing rapidly with the increasing popularity of endurance riding and breeding. A registered horse has, to some degree, been proven as endurance quality stock. To be registered, a horse must have finished in the top ten in an approved race of 35 miles or more, with a minimum of 50 contestants. Registry is also given to any horse that successfully completes 250 miles of approved rides within one year. And finally, any foal of two registered horses is allowed registry.

Feeding and General Care

A clean environment, adequate rest and relaxation, good nutrition, regular exercise, and grooming must generally accompany the more rigorous aspects of conditioning and training if you and your horse want to achieve maximum performance. The horse's stable area should be kept clean. Be sure there are no protruding nails or holes in the flooring and no other potential hazards. Although a roof shelter is not mandatory for a horse's well-being (they lived under the sky for centuries), the corral area should be such that it will not confine the horse to standing continually in deep mud during the rainy season. During the fly season, you should do your best to make your horse comfortable by effective use of fly repellents. There are several varieties on the market that can be used both directly on the horse and around his

*Ann Hyland, *Endurance Riding* (New York: J. B. Lippincott, 1975), p. 22.

living area. Manure should not be spread, but piled and stored so the heat of fermentation will help destroy parasites and their eggs. Avoid throwing hay feed on or near the manure. It is preferable to build an elevated feeder. This is especially worthwhile as it cuts down feed waste. Clean water, from an automatic waterer or a trough, should be available at all times.

Horses are particularly vulnerable to parasites, and many problems can result from parasite infestation in the endurance horse. A good worming program is essential. The program should be initiated by a veterinarian, but you can administer commercial worming medication yourself on a regular basis. If parasites or worms are suspected for problems such as weight loss or low energy in spite of medication, you should have your veterinarian administer blood and fecal specimen tests to determine the actual type of parasite that may be causing the problem.

In caring for your horse, I recommend the liberal use of a good veterinarian. Not only should you use a vet for regular vaccinations and tube worming but you also might want to take advantage of his ability to help evaluate the horse's body chemistry. Disease prevention and overall performance can be enhanced by identifying changes as they occur in blood chemistry before they manifest themselves. Using blood tests to determine nutritional needs in horses is not a new concept. Many top endurance riders have used blood tests to evaluate their horse's comparative condition before, during, and after training. By so doing, a more accurate determination of vitamin and mineral needs can be made. Horses must receive a quality diet that provides enough nutrients to compensate for the extreme work they will be asked to perform.

It should be noted that blood tests for horses should be compared to baselines, and not general norms. Endurance horses are likely to have readings that are significantly different than those that have been prepared as standards for less athletic animals. It also should be noted that since a horse manufactures its own vitamins, mineral deficiencies will be more likely to occur than vitamin deficiencies except in cases of extreme stress. The best source of vitamins and minerals is food. (If supplements are used, add them to the horse's diet gradually and take care the horse doesn't refuse his regular food.) Blood tests and evaluations are an effective way to determine ideal nutritional needs and prevent deficiencies, but nothing can take the place of close and continual observation of your horse's appearance and performance. This will be a primary concern during specific training, but you also should be aware of signs of discontentment your horse might exhibit in general. If he acts restless or eats poorly, it may be a sign of poor feed. If his coat turns dull and his eyes lose their pink color, he may need a mineral supplement. You should observe the horse constantly for indications of pain, whether caused by a digestive disorder or some external problem.

There are many different signs of impending health problems in the horse. For example, difficulty in breathing, heaves, and a lack of stamina can be a sign of dusty, dry hay. Forefoot lameness and muscular cramps can be a sign of overfeeding grains during periods of inactivity. Cribbing (eating the wood around the barn or fence) is sometimes a sign of calcium or phosphorous need. The many indications of general health problems are not within the scope of this book. In order to become more knowledgeable about the subject, I recommend adding two excellent books, *Horses and Horsemanship,* and *How to Recognize Horse Health Problems* to your library.* The important thing is to make a conscientious effort to observe the horse's performance, manners, and appearance.

Proper Feeding

What is a proper feeding program for a prospective Ride & Tie horse? Fortunately, the answer is not quite as complex as it is in dealing with our feeding program. This may be because horses are not equipped with those characteristics that have complicated our dietary habits—they are content to thrive on nature's most basic products. The simplicity of a feeding program for horses, however, is somewhat compli-

*Bill Weikel, ed., *How to Recognize Horse Health Problems* (Alhambra, Calif.: Borden, 1976); and M. E. Ensminger, *Horses and Horsemanship* (Danville, Ill.: Interstate, 1977).

cated by the extreme physical demands that will be placed on the horse during training for Ride & Tie. Lack of natural grazing also requires the feeding program to be more carefully evaluated. But, with some basic knowledge, observation, and experimentation, you can easily master the art of feeding an endurance horse.

To start the feeding program for a newly acquired animal, you should continue the same type of schedule and feed to which the horse was previously accustomed. As he becomes adjusted to his new environment and increased work load, you can make a gradual change in his diet if you feel such a change is necessary. Sudden changes in a horse's diet cause gastric disturbances quite easily. This should be brought to mind when temporarily trailering the horse to new places. In such instances, it is best to bring his regular food from home. With some exceptions, the more routine the horse's day, the more content he is. A regular feeding schedule is especially important. A horse fed at approximately the same time each day will be more relaxed and confident in his home. This regularity should not, however, be carried to extremes. Varying the time within one or two hours will teach your horse a little patience without making him nervous. This way, in case you are late for an occasional feeding, he will not develop bad habits such as pawing the ground or kicking at his feeder.

Deciding what to feed the horse is rather uncomplicated. There is grass, alfalfa hay, and oat hay. There are grains including oats, barley, and corn. Concentrated foods and commercially mixed feeds are also available. The choice or combination best for your horse is largely dependent on the individual horse. The type of feed the horse was raised on, his unique rate of metabolism, and his internal physiological uniqueness will combine to specify a rationing of feed and feed choices. This will probably be different than for any other horse. Experimentation with individuality and optimum performance must be based on certain guidelines.

First of all, your horse's feed must be clean and fresh. Musty, dusty grains, and overly dry hay from poor soil will not offer the horse the proper nutrients. When you buy hay, you should inquire about the quality from other horsemen. Grains should be stored in containers with lids and should be checked periodically for mold and rancidity. Whenever possible, the horse should be allowed to graze on rich, green foliage. If regular pasture is not available, just stopping at grassy areas during daily rides for fifteen to twenty minutes can be beneficial. (Augmenting your horse's diet with some fresh vegetables, such as carrots, is a good idea.)

Secondly, the proper proportions of concentrated foods and roughage should be given to the horse. During heavy training, the horse will require relatively more concentrates and grains and less roughage. During lighter work, the horse should eat more hay and less grain. On infrequent days off, the horse can be given a ration of bran the night before the day of rest in place of the reduction in grain. If you are working the horse hard and feeding him high amounts of concentrates and small amounts of hay, be careful to note if he is cribbing. If he is, it indicates a need for more roughage. If his performance and health are fine and he still eats wood, it may be that he is just bored. It must be remembered that horses are grazing animals and accustomed to eating almost constantly. If the horse is feeding on the ground, place the hay in various locations so that he has to move around to eat it all.

The same problem can occur if you are feeding your horse concentrated hay pellets or cubes instead of hay. Although this manner of feed combines both concentrated protein and roughage, and it is a convenient way of feeding and storing hay, the horse can become bored because pellets are eaten more quickly than hay. If you choose this type feed you might try either spreading them out on the ground, or, if you are using a feeder, placing a few small stones with the pellets to make it more difficult for him to eat. You also might throw a couple of pounds of straw in his stable to keep him occupied during the night.

Care should be taken to feed your horse in relation to the amount of work he is doing. The syndrome known as *tying up* in horses, which is often related to overgraining, can be a serious threat to the horse's health. *Tying up* describes a muscle rigidity and lameness that usually affects the loins and rump. The problem actually results from an excessive build-up of lactic acid, often indicated by brown-colored urine.

The exact relationship between excessive grain and tying up is not completely understood. It should be remembered that weakness of the muscles often reflects irregularity and fatigue of the bowels. If the problem occurs, keep the animal moving, allowing him to eat or drink along the way. Prevention of the problem, however, seems closer related to training than to feed.

If a horse is lacking energy or losing weight he may not be receiving enough energy for the demands placed on him. You might try gradually introducing the horse to cracked corn. Pound for pound, corn furnishes more energy than most other grains. Corn should not be a replacement for crimped oats because the oats have more complete nutrients. It should be noted that it is suggested that these grains be cracked or crimped. This is to assure that the maximum amount of nutrition is obtained from them. Although the horse can metabolize cellulose, grains that are not properly crushed will pass through the body and provide no nutrition. The crushed grains are easily digested, even by horses with good, even teeth.

The horse's diet should be adhered to consistently throughout training right up to race time. A "super" diet for a race, such as carbohydrate-loading is not as effective as a continual balanced diet. A balanced diet should include as wide a variety of foods as possible. Irregular mixtures of oat hay and alfalfa hay, corn, oats, mixed feed, occasional carrots, and such will assure that the horse is receiving proper vitamins and minerals. This diet also will minimize problems relating to dietary changes unavoidable during travel. The amount of food should vary with increases in training effort and weather conditions. For example, during a race it may be necessary to administer more electrolytes to the horse than is normally given him during less intense work and heat conditions. (Even in this case, the electrolytes should be given in very small proportions so as not to upset gastrointestinal functioning. Electrolytes also should be given choice free as opposed to force feeding or mixing with grain.)

Foot Care and Shoes

The horse's foot and shoes are the next most important prerequisite for injury-free conditioning. Not only will the horse have to run over many miles of rocky terrain, but he also must carry the weight of a saddle and rider. Such activity may be slightly beyond what nature intended for the hooves to handle. The importance of good shoes and a good *farrier* cannot be stressed enough.* Ideally, the hoof should be deep and wide and the angle of the hoof from the coronet to the ground should be about forty-five degrees. The wall of the hoof should be at least ¼ inch thick at the heel to about ½ inch at the toe. There should be a good concave arch in the sole so that the frog (a pad in the middle of the sole) actually touches the ground. If it doesn't touch the ground, the arch will not adequately support the weight of the horse as it was designed. Also, blood circulation will not be as efficient as it should. This is because there is a plantar cushion just above the frog, composed of a network of capillaries, that pump blood back up toward the heart.

This is the basic description of the hoof you will want to maintain when you shoe the horse. Except when corrective shoeing is necessary, the shoe should be a mere extension of the foot. Although a horse with severe corrective shoeing needs should not have been considered as a Ride & Tie horse, minor shoe improvisations are common and not too disruptive. Very often, for example, an Arabian will forge (kick his front feet with his rear feet). This is because the Arabian is short coupled with long legs. To cure this problem, have your farrier increase the angle of the front hooves a little more than normal by leaving extra heel and taking off a little toe. This will make the horse break over a little faster. On the rear feet, there should be a little less angle than normal by leaving the toe normal and taking off a little heel. This will leave a little more foot on the ground and will slightly delay lift-off. Then, on the rear hooves, have your farrier put on rim shoes. Rim shoes have more surface area for better traction and also are lighter. The lighter the shoe, the longer it stays on the ground because the horse doesn't lift the foot as high or as far as he would with the heavier shoe. Staying on the ground longer will keep the horse from kicking his front legs with his rear legs.

*A *farrier* is a blacksmith who shoes horses.

A well-cared for horse needs a skillful farrier. Until you are confident that your horse is being shod well, you can start observing obvious shoeing errors that might be made. For example, you should note the front feet are both the same size and the rear feet are equal to each other. The toes should be the same height and the heels should be the same height. Look at the angle of the foot. The axis of the foot should extend equally into the axis of the pastern. Normally, this will be about 45 degrees. The clinches should be smooth and the foot should have no sharp edges. However, be sure that the hoof is not filed down too close to meeting the shoe. The shoe should be a little wider and longer than the foot on the outside and rest evenly on its bearing surface. Finally, there should be as little nailing as possible. Three on each side of the hoof should do the job. The nails should start in low and come out high. Your horse should be shod about every six weeks. Shoes prevent the hoof from wearing down naturally and then will thus grow about one-half inch a month. If the hoof is allowed to grow too long, tendon strain, corns, and splitting hooves can result. Riding with overworn shoes increases the chances of the horse throwing a shoe and coming up lame. To assure that you don't let too much time elapse between shoeings, it is a good idea to set up a long-range schedule with your farrier.

Check advertisements for horseshoes other than the traditional ones made of steel. Urethane boots, for example, can be put on and off of the horse as they are needed. They provide padding and cushioning under the sole and allow the horse to roam unshod when he is not being ridden. This type of shoe may or may not be suitable for your particular needs. It is good for the development of the horse's feet if he is allowed to run unshod most of the time. This is only ideal, however, if the horse is roaming in good pasture with variable terrain, good sod, and natural ponds or creeks. As for under-sole padding, this is helpful in preventing stone bruises that may occur on rocky trails. It should be noted that neoprene pads are also placed under metal shoes. So, it is likely the only advantage of the neoprene boots for the horse confined to a corral existence is the lack of nail holes in the hoof. But this may be offset by lack of ventilation and the rubbing of the coronet that can be a problem with the boots. (If you do let your horse roam unshod during the rainy season, the boots are convenient for those occasional rides.)

Many new products have recently come on the market, including a vibrathane horseshoe called the Flex-Step. The claim of the manufacturer is that Flex-Step weighs one-quarter of the same size steel shoe and will last twice as long. They also claim that the shock transmitted to the horse's legs is 75 percent less than steel shoes tested under the same conditions. Unfortunately, however, many farriers claim the shoe is too flexible for adequate support in endurance riding and that it loosens quite easily.

So, unless you are experimenting with alternatives, you probably will be using the standard metal horseshoes. I recommend Diamond's Saddle-lite, as it is lighter and better for endurance horses. Be sure to carefully observe the horse's performance as it relates to his footwear regardless of the shoe. Take care of his shoes and his feet just as meticulously as you take care of your own.

Training and Conditioning

With the knowledge of basic horse care under your belt, you can now initiate the more advanced training schedule for a Ride & Tie. It is here that the parallel between the human runner and the horse is the most pronounced. In fact, the same rules of training you should be adhering to can be applied to the horse: develop a fitness base; increase stress factors gradually; don't overtrain; and monitor and evaluate performance regularly.

If your horse is starting out as a beginning "athlete," the first month or two should be devoted to gradual adaptation to being ridden regularly. You should start out by *longeing* the horse at the end of a rope (or *longe line*) for ten to twenty minutes at a time.* This will start his conditioning and get him acquainted with verbal commands as he circles around you. If you have a wide area and a long enough rope, you can move him out in a lope. Otherwise, keep him on variations of the trot and occasionally reverse his direction. If he has not been trained to do this, a long stick or whip threatening

*A *longe line* (or longeing rein) is a rein or strap used to lead or guide a horse in training.

him from behind will start him moving. Bringing him to a stop by commanding "whoa," with a slight tug on the lead rope, should be followed by a rewarding pat on the neck and an occasional treat such as a carrot or an apple.

Rides in this early part of training should be limited to about five miles at a speed of about five miles per hour. Walk alongside him when going up or down steep hills until he begins to muscle up and lose fat. If hills are new to him, he will get enough of a workout without you on his back. Working alongside him this way will train him to run alongside you in a race. He should be taught to walk or run at a pace that will keep his shoulder even with your side. This will enable you to watch him and will also prevent him from stepping on your heels.

Running alongside your horse in this manner is a convenient way to exercise yourself and the horse at the same time. The horse need not be saddled. Working with only a halter from the ground will help train him to use the halter alone when you are aboard. You should be able to run alongside the horse's shoulder from about three feet away so enough slack remains in the lead line to allow you freedom of movement in your running. (It will look like you are walking a large dog.) You should also practice holding on to his mane while walking, trotting, and running uphill. As the horse's condition progresses, he will be able to pull you up the hill.

Running alongside the horse offers variety in training and competition. It also allows both runner and horse to train together. (Scotty Ray Morris)

Tailing a horse up a hill, in training and competition, is beneficial to both the horse and runner, as long as the horse has been properly trained to do it. (Scotty Ray Morris)

Although this will take effort, it will be easier on the horse than if you were on his back and easier on you than if you were running without assistance. On extremely steep and narrow trails "tailing" the horse may be the only way to safely ascend. On such trails it is often impossible to go two abreast, too strenuous to ride, and somewhat dangerous to lead the horse.

To train your horse to tail, he must first become accustomed to having you behind him, handling and pulling on his tail. Then, using the lead line to drive him, steer him while holding the tip of the rope along with the tip of his tail. You will find that the horse will often attempt to turn toward the side of the lead line and will try to head back down the hill. Try to catch him before he makes his turn by motioning him forward and stepping off to the side he is turning toward. Keep a firm grip on the lead line. Don't get overconfident with your horse's willingness to tail straight up a hill so he pulls you up without using the lead rope. I did this once, thinking the hill was steep enough to keep him moving at a slow pace. I didn't expect a sudden dip in the hill. Unable to keep up with the horse on the downslope, but determined not to lose him, I was dragged fifty feet until he was forced to slow down part way up the next hill. I managed to get back to my feet and work my way up to the halter rope feeling more scared than hurt.

Once a good base is established via the light riding and longeing, you may want to have a complete blood test taken to determine the horse's chemical health profile before you start more rigorous work. Blood evaluations, however, are only meaningful when compared to an apparently healthy baseline. If you have been able to improve the looks and spirit of your horse with the light conditioning program, but have not yet put the more demanding stresses on him, the chances are that his level of health will provide a good baseline. You should also keep accurate records of your horse's performance and physiological measurement. Measurements should include pulse and respiration rate, time out, type of terrain, previous feeding (type, quantity, and time), amount of water consumed during the ride, and attitude and willingness. In order to make these records more meaningful, it is helpful to periodically use a specified course that will be ridden in a specified time. By taking pulse and respiration both at the completion of the course and at two-minute intervals, conditioning progress can be determined. If pulse rates are higher on one day on the same course and in the same time (assuming weather and humidity are similar), then you can look to possible explanations such as overtraining, inadequate rest, or dietary irregularities.

As training and conditioning progress, you will eventually be taking longer rides. You may even want to compete in some of the trail and endurance rides that are advertised in various riding magazines such as *Saddle Action*. These rides are conducted with regular veterinarian checks along the way, as is done in Ride & Tie, to safeguard your horse's health.

Until you and your horse become confident in each other's competitive ability, attitude, and condition, these rides should be considered training rides. Furthermore, postride care of your horse should provide ample rest before hard training is resumed. If the horse was pushed hard, a minimum of five days rest is recommended. This rest, however, should include light exercise either with a longe line or by running alongside him.

When riding the longer training rides of twenty-five to fifty miles or more, you should stop every fifteen or twenty minutes to determine the horse's ability to continue without undue stress. Not only will this assure that the horse is not overworked, but it will also serve in getting him accustomed to frequent stopping, as in Ride & Tie. To provide you with a guideline that will help you determine the horse's ability to continue, I have provided a recovery index that has been formulated by Dr. James Steere, who has experienced Ride & Tie as both a participant and a veterinarian. Following such an index is important for several reasons:

a. The index measures the speed of pulse and respiration recovery. The rate of recovery in Ride & Tie is more important than the pulse count.

b. The index measures condition based on gut sounds. Gut sounds are probably the most important single sign in measuring condition. When the horse is at rest, the gut sounds, due to peristaltic motion of the intestines, are almost constant. As the horse tires, blood is diverted from the gut to the survival organs. The gut sounds slow down until, in the exhausted horse, they are totally absent.

c. The index attempts to give a measure of the horse's hydration. This is based on the skin pinch test, given at the shoulder of the animal.

All three measurements are scored with a maximum of 10 points for a horse in excellent condition, to 0 for a completely exhausted horse.

It should be remembered that this is only a guideline, but it is as dependable at the 70/70 requirement used on most endurance rides and Ride & Tie events. (The 70/70 requirement means the horse is not allowed to leave a Vet Check until

THE RECOVERY INDEX

PULSE	RECOVERY		PULSE	RECOVERY		PULSE	RECOVERY	
15 sec.	10%	20%	15 sec.	10%	20%	15 sec.	10%	20%
40	36	32	31	28	25	22	20	18
39	35	31	30	27	24	21	19	17
38	34	30	29	26	23	20	18	16
37	33	30	28	25	22	19	17	15
36	32	29	27	24	21	18	16	14
35	31	28	26	23	21	17	15	14
34	31	27	25	22	20	16	14	13
33	30	26	24	22	19	15	13	12
32	29	26	23	21	18			

RECOVERY INDEX—SCALE 0 to 10

Pulse-Respiration Recovery Time

4 points	20% in 5 minutes. Respiration lower than pulse.
3 points	10% in 5 minutes. Respiration lower than pulse.
2 points	20% in 10 minutes. Respiration lower than pulse.
1 point	10% in 10 minutes. Respiration lower than pulse.
0 points	No recovery in 10 minutes. Respiration higher than pulse.

Gut Sounds

3 points	Almost constant rumbling, gurgling, and "gassing."
2 points	Moderate to good sounds every 20-30 seconds.
1 point	Barely audible—about one per minute.
0 points	Absent.

Hydration

3 points	Normal (pick up fold of skin at point of shoulder, release; skin will flatten immediately).
2 points	Slight dehydration—skin fold flattens in about 5 seconds.
1 point	Moderate dehydration—skin fold flattens in about 10 seconds.
0 points	Severe dehydration—skin fold remains; no saliva; eyes have "sunken" look.

SCORE	WHAT DO?
10	GO!
7-9	Go. Just watch low score parameter.
5-6	Proceed with caution.
3-4	Walk horse to nearest vet.
0 (in any category)	Wait for recovery and return of energy before proceeding.
0 (in all 3)	Do not move horse. Get veterinarian now.

OTHER REASONS FOR HOLDING FOR RECOVERY
1. Temperature over 103° F (respiration will remain high).
2. Lame.
3. "Out of gas" (very low energy level).
4. "Thumps."
5. Totally relaxed anal sphincter.
6. Other signs of exhaustion.

The 10% and 20% figures in the Recovery Index indicate the drop in pulse rate at five minute intervals. The index, introduced by Dr. James Steere in 1976, was originally published in *Saddle Action* magazine April 1977. It is reprinted with permission from Dr. Steere and *Saddle Action* magazine.

its pulse rate is 70 and its respiration is 70 per minute. At rest the horse's pulse rate should be about 32-40 beats per minute and his respiration should be about 8-15 breaths per minute.) The pulse can be taken at the base of the tail, the inside of the knee, or under the jaw. Watch the nostrils and flanks move to count respirations. A stethoscope is helpful for listening to the heart and gut sounds.

Figuring the amount of effort the horse should exert for optimum training efficiency should follow the same procedure used to determine your own work load. Comparing day to day performance is best, but signs of stress may not be obvious to you all the time. It is best to prevent overstress by working the horse aerobically. The recovery index is only helpful in assuring that he is able to pay off an oxygen debt before he continues. Unfortunately, as of this writing, target heart rate formulas for exercising horses aerobically have not yet been devised. But for some time I have been experimenting with apparent maximum attainable heart rates of horses (at maximum efforts on steep inclines), correlating the results with the horses' ages and applying the modified human target heart rate formula. I have come close to a formula that will dictate a training heart rate for horses. Based on the intuitive judgment of riders who know their horses well enough to know when they are working aerobically, the formulas, in most instances, correlated well with pulse rates taken during such paces. The formula is: 200 minus (the horse's age multiplied by 4) minus the horse's resting pulse rate times 60 percent plus the resting pulse rate. For example, if the horse is eleven years of age and has a resting pulse rate of 40, his pulse rate would be:

$$200 - 44 (156) - 40 (116) \times 0.60 (70) + 40$$
$$= 110 \text{ beats per minute.}$$

Using this number as a target heart rate may be a fair indication of a training pace for your horse. In the beginning, stop the horse periodically to take his pulse to assure he is at the right heart rate. As his condition improves, his respiration will become synchronized with his pulse rate. Then, to determine his heart rate, you need only count his respiration. That can be done without leaving the saddle.

Furthermore, a well-conditioned horse will tend to achieve a pulse and respiration rate equal to the pace he is running. By counting how many times the left forefoot strikes the ground, you can approximate the heart rate at which the horse is working. By riding at a pace equal to the 60 percent target heart rate, you will be working the horse aerobically, assuming his respiration is not exceeding the pace.

Riding the horse for long, slow distance at a steady state, or aerobic, intensity is the best way to keep a horse from tying up during a race or hard training session. If a horse is worked regularly at an anaerobic intensity, then allowed to rest for a day or two, then ridden anaerobically again, he is prone to this tying up syndrome. It is brought on when the dissipation of lactic acid from the muscle tissue reaches a stage, at about forty hours, that causes the muscle to be unprepared for further anaerobic work that will result in additional increases in lactic acid. This problem can be avoided by riding the horse every day, getting him used to irregular exercise sessions, or keeping the lactic acid at a minimum with aerobic work.

Various Gaits

There are various opinions on the type of gait that should be used with regard to the effort exerted in training and during Ride & Tie racing. Most endurance riders claim it is best to maintain an extended trot during the majority of the race. A trot is good for the horse because it spreads the work load more evenly than usually happens in the canter or lope. So fatigue is minimized and the concussion to the legs is not as severe. Some trainers never allow their horses to go beyond a trot unless they run all out in a blinding gallop. In this way the horse learns he must either pace himself at a good trot or sprint. Nothing in between is allowed. The horse is urged on in the trot until he has reached a speed just below where he would have to break into a run. With gradual training, the horse can usually be taught to extend into a smooth, consistent, ten-mile-an-hour trot. If you are going to train your horse to run a race in this manner, you also have to discipline yourself to keep him from breaking into a lope. It will take discipline because the lope is usually more comfortable and enjoyable for you as a beginning rider. But, if you are not consistent during training, it will be more difficult to keep your horse at a trot when urging him to go faster. Thus, the beginning stages of training should include walking and steady trotting.

Working a horse continually at an extended trot is, however, not the only way to ride a race. Once again, the individuality of the horse is the variable factor. Some horses have a smooth, collected lope that is actually more efficient than their extended trot at comparable speeds. It would be more efficient, for such a horse, if the Ride & Tie strategy called for the horse to be tied at relatively short intervals. In order to determine which way your horse will work best, first give him his head on a long course to determine his natural preference is. (Do not rely totally on this because what he would do naturally is not necessarily the same as what he will do with you on his back.) The best way to determine the most efficient pace is to time him on a specified course loping, and record his pulse and respiration along with two two-minute recovery rates. Then, train him to travel an extended trot and time him at a trot over the same course, taking the same measurements. Each time you run or trot the horse over the course, determine his pace/heart rate and compare it to the projected target heart rate. Once you have all the data and observations recorded, you can evaluate it and come to a conclusion. Whatever you decide, be sure that your partner, and anyone else who may be helping you exercise the horse, all train the horse in the manner you prescribe. Otherwise, the horse never learns how to pace a race efficiently.

Having other people available to help you and your partner condition your horse is a good idea, providing they are good riders and obey your instructions. Extra people are helpful if you have a second horse that needs to be trained and conditioned to replace your horse in case he is injured. Having a backup horse available is just as important as having an alternate teammate available. In fact, if all goes well with your original team, the backup horse can be used in the event by the alternate runner and whatever teammate he is able to find. Using the backup horse in training affords an opportunity to train your horse to be led by another horse. This practice can be used to give your horse a change of pace in training and will give him the versatility that a good horse should have.

Variety is an important aspect of advanced Ride & Tie training for your horse. Although a horse prefers consistency in his feeding schedule and regularity in his training lessons, he should be subjected to varying types of terrain, environments, and other horses. Occasional rides amidst other horses will prevent him from becoming too nervous on race day and keep up his competitive spirit. Introducing him to new environments and terrains has its obvious advantages. In the 1977 Olema Ride & Tie, for example, one horse had never been exposed to the ocean surf before the race. When it came to a section of the course that paralleled the Pacific Ocean, the horse shied away from the surf and the rider was forced to ride him closer to the inland cliffs where the sand was much deeper and more difficult to move in. Although the stretch was only about 1½ miles, the horse overworked itself in the deep sand and had to be walked up the hill when leaving the beach.

Another good reason for varying the terrain and trails during training is that it teaches the horse to pay attention to where he is going. A horse that rides the same trail continually will eventually start to take his eyes off the trail and "daydream." The variety will keep him from getting stale and he will be more likely to look to the next day's workout with enthusiasm and interest. If new trails are difficult to find, take him on unexpected shortcuts over embankments and through creeks. Taking such paths increases the chances of coming across new and unfamiliar objects that might frighten the horse. Increased familiarity with such objects will cause him to be safer to ride on a race in which such objects could be encountered.

When a horse shies away from something, gently turn him so that he is facing the object. Calm him down and reassure him that everything is all right. If you can see what it is he is fearful of, walk him past it, allowing him to keep his head and eyes turned to the object. Don't force him close to it or punish him for acting skittish. Continue walking past the object several times each time you ride that trail. Eventually, he will overcome the fear and you will be able to lope past the object without consequence. If, however, he continues to shy away from the object after a period of time, even though you are fairly sure that he is no longer afraid of it, then disciplinary action is in order. At this point, you should keep the reins held firmly as you pass the object and keep him pointed straight, being as harsh with him as is necessary to keep him straight. Soon, you will be able to tell the difference between a scared horse and a bad habit.

When riding over various terrains, you should encourage your horse to drink out of as many different clean water sources as possible—creeks, streams, ponds, rivers, lakes, troughs, hoses, and puddles. The horse should be allowed to drink as much water as he desires on a long ride. (You should not, however, allow an exhausted horse to eat until his circulation returns to normal.) By teaching him to drink out of various sources, he will be less likely to balk at important water sources when it is needed during a race. Conditioning, acclimating your horse to heat, and furnishing him with sufficient water and electrolytes will increase your chances of successfully finishing a Ride & Tie.

Hill Riding

Once your horse has reached a good fitness base and has been ridden on the trails for a while, you can start riding him on the hills. Up until now, you should have been riding him up the hills at a walk or travelling alongside him. You should also be confident of his ability to tail you up hills and steep draws. Your own conditioning should be such that you are able to follow your horse up hills easily. In spite of the fact that you will spend a lot of time running alongside your horse on hills during competition, your horse should also be expected to carry you up hills rapidly. The pace at which you ride your horse up a hill is subject to the same variables that determine the pace of your running. Although it is usually recommended to trot a horse uphill, keeping him on a straight course, you must also take into consideration the slope of the hills and the inclination of the horse. By giving him his head on different hills, you will find that sometimes he prefers to take a hill in short lunges, supporting the majority of his weight on his rear legs and jumping from section to section. He will probably do this on inclines steeper than 50 percent grade. Depending on his condition and his familiarity with the hill, he may be more efficient loping up the hill than trotting. If the horse does not know how long the hill will be, it is up to you to pace him correctly, assuming you are familiar with the hill. In such cases, you should pace him according to his target heart rate and be sensitive to a loss of energy and strength in his rear legs. Most importantly, ride light and forward in the saddle when you are riding a horse up a hill fast. Use your weight to help him. When you think he is starting to fatigue, ride him at angles to the hill, slow him down or get off and run alongside, but never stop him. If he learns that he can be intimidated by a hill and end the struggle by stopping, he will never make the Ride & Tie horse you want him to be.

Downhill runs will vary in pace with the angle of slope. On extreme inclines you should hold on to his mane and walk alongside him. If the ground is loose with deep dirt and shale, however, you can stay on and slide him down. On moderately steep inclines you can either trot or lope depending on which gait your horse prefers. You should remember that going downhill usually results in more shock to the horse's legs, and every effort should be made to maintain an even, rhythmic stride. As a horse nears the bottom of the hill, he should be allowed to gradually break into a faster pace while you lift yourself up in the saddle. Lifting yourself will help minimize gravitational impact and the increased pace will keep stressful braking action to a minimum, as well as giving the horse momentum for the next hill.

When riding your horse down a long, moderately sloping hill, it is important to realize exactly how fast you are going. Otherwise, a chain reaction can occur that can put you in trouble. First, you realize that you have gained too much speed. This can be frightening when you are running down a hill too fast. But on a horse the sense of panic is somewhat more pervading. The horse, being extremely sensitive to any sign of fear felt by its rider and already a bit apprehensive about the speed he is travelling, now becomes panic stricken. He may try to outrun the hill, setting his head and ignoring any attempt to restrain him. Riding a runaway horse down a hill in this manner is dangerous to both of you and all attempts to prevent the situation should be considered. To prevent this, always maintain a safe speed and concentrate on the pace as it relates to the terrain. It also helps to maintain a confident, relaxed attitude at all times. This applies even if you are rounding a bend adjacent to a thousand-foot drop-off. Focusing too much attention on the situation will begin to worry the horse and could initiate the chain reaction. This is especially important when riding a sensitive Arabian. One day I was loping an Arabian down a hill using only a halter and a loose-cinched saddle. I had lost my concentration for a moment and was enjoying the beautiful scenery. Just as I realized that we were moving a little too fast, the slope suddenly took a steep dip and my saddle slipped forward slightly. The surprise caused me to tense suddenly and I must have registered enough anxiety to permeate through to the horse. Just as I started to slow him down, he increased his speed and lowered his head, totally ignoring my commands. Realizing the importance of a relaxed attitude in such a predicament, I settled back, gave the horse his head, and started whistling. I continued whistling for what seemed like ages, hiding the fact that I was scared to death. After a few moments, I gently pulled back on the lead rope and said, "Whoa." The horse, convinced by my performance, slowed immediately to a halt. (To this day, I can't remember the tune I was whistling.)

Preparing for Competition

Assuming the horse was adequately trained by the fall and you commenced your actual training and conditioning program around January, the horse should be averaging three rides a week in late March, each of about three hours duration. Preferably these will be Ride & Tie rides with the partner you will be using in the race. Unless the horse shows signs of overwork, mileage should be close to race pace. Most likely there will be a need for increased feed rations by this time to compensate for the increased work. Early April is a good time for another worming and another blood test to compare to the original baseline. In the blood test, which is similar to your own chemistry profile, you and the vet will look for significant changes and attempt to rectify the cause.

Within a month or so of the planned Ride & Tie, it is a good idea to trailer your horse to the sight of the course, if such a trip is possible. If the race is well organized, the course should be marked by this time. Familiarizing yourself with the course on the prerides will help you plan your strategy and generally let you know what you will be up against. It is also advantageous if the horse has an opportunity to learn the course. In this way the terrain will become familiar to him and he will be less likely to spook or become nervous. Furthermore, he will learn that he can get home on the course by continuing to go forward. This will give him a psychological advantage over other horses who do not ride the entire course until race day. And finally, preriding the course will make you less likely to get lost on race day.

If travelling to a race will be the horse's first time in a trailer, be sure ahead of time that the horse has been trained to trailer. Borrow someone's trailer during training and see how he does. If you find that the horse does not trailer easily, try not to force him at first. Instead, tie him to the trailer for an hour or so until he no longer fears it. Then, tie him to the travelling hitch inside the trailer on a long enough rope to allow him to get in and out of the trailer on his own. Make sure that he knows there is grain inside and watch him so he doesn't trip himself on the lead rope. If this doesn't work, throw a rope around his rump, with someone on either side to pull him into the trailer. When travelling, make sure his head is tied so that he can't get turned around in the trailer and injure himself.

When you and your partner Ride & Tie in an unfamiliar area where other horses are being ridden, your horse may try to pull away when he is tied. If so, take extra care to make a secure tie and calm the horse down before you continue on your run. If the horse continues pulling hard enough to free or injure himself, you will have to train him to break the habit. The best way to do this is to run a rope with a slip loop around his girth. Then, run the rope through his front legs, up through the halter ring and tie it high to a tree fork or limb. When the horse pulls back, the rope will tighten and cause him to step forward to relieve the pressure around his girth. It shouldn't take too long for him to realize that pulling is not going to do any good. Also, if you ride often with other horses, he will eventually get used to horses passing by.

Training your horse to tie, to trailer, to pass strange objects, and to slide down hills are just a few examples of the challenges you face in preparing your horse for Ride & Tie. You should realize that each horse has his own inadequacies and fears. To overcome the problems, you will have to rely on your own imagination, patience, and understanding, in addition to the experience of other horse trainers. The combined challenges of training and conditioning in Ride & Tie may seem incredibly demanding, but the difficulty is relative to what you are accustomed. Marty Jensen, for example, claims that a Ride & Tie is no more exhausting than a typical

The horse must be trained to tie at a spot where horses and runners pass by. He also should be trained to be calm around other horses. (Scotty Ray Morris)

day at home. Marty is the female half of a husband-wife team, from Portland, Oregon, that is a top contender each year in the National Ride & Tie. She takes care of her husband, seven children, thirty rabbits, three horses, two goats, and a house without bending to the demands of running fifty miles a week, riding seventy-five miles a week, and training her own horses.

In fact, most Ride & Tie participants have busy schedules and active life-styles. It seems that physical fitness is more time-producing than time-consuming. People who make time to take care of themselves usually make time for other things.

8
Strategy and Tactics

The brain is complex
And needs to be taxed
To perform with high quality.
But war is a mess,
And though I do enjoy chess,
Ride & Tie is my "cup of tea."

Planning and practicing a Ride & Tie strategy is the final state of training. An overall game plan will put enough method in the madness and chaos of a race to at least give you a good start. However, the many variables that occur in Ride & Tie often make adhering to the original strategy impossible. Make sure you remain flexible.

The Need for Strategy

Flexibility in your strategy is firmly acknowledged by national champion Ken Williams. Williams, a Santa Cruz, California, teacher, had been nicknamed "Computer Ken" because he used a computer to determine an ideal Ride & Tie strategy. His strategy was designed to use the individual capabilities of each team member. For one particular race, the plan was formulated to allow Williams to run up most of the hills, and for his partner to run down the hills. Each man would be doing the most of what he was best suited to do. As it actually happened, however, Williams ran down most of the hills and his partner ran up most of the hills. The horse upset the plan at the first Vet Check because he had been so excited by the start that it took him fifteen minutes longer to recover than planned. (In spite of the discarded strategy, Williams and his partner, Don Roth, of Menlo Park, California, were flexible enough to win the race.)

Rick Sylvester will attest that the best laid plans of Ride & Tie often go astray. Rick, whose talents keep him busy as a writer, stunt man, mountain guide, ski instructor, and film producer (as well as doubling for Roger Moore in several James Bond movies), had his Ride & Tie plans upset three years in a row. He had to run most of his first race because his horse was declared lame at the first Vet Check. For his second Ride & Tie, the stage was set for victory. The race was to be held in his own neighborhood of Squaw Valley, California, giving him a "home-court advantage." Also, he had a partner who had run a two-mile steeplechase in 9:07. However, the day before the race his partner claimed to have sprained an ankle. Sylvester felt the injury occurred partly because of his partner's fear of horses: "The fact our horse boasted only one eye and Cliff Lewis (the owner of the horse) had cautioned something about passing runners only on the right (or was it the left?) might have exercised a certain deleterious effect on his confidence." Fortunately, or so it seemed, a last-minute partner, who had competed with Olympic high-jumper Dwight Stones at Long Beach State, turned up for Rick, and the race was started in fine form. At about six miles out, Rick made his last tie. Several miles later a riderless horse went galloping by him with a large number 9 painted on its flanks. It was the one-eyed horse. Someone had untied it by mistake. That race over, Rick prepared for the 1977 Levi's Ride & Tie with Ron Nehring, a former AAU National half-mile champion. Unfortunately, Ron had not ridden a horse in a year and halfway through the race his legs from ankle to crotch "were like strips of red, raw and bleeding meat." In spite of the pain, he continued as best he could and afforded Sylvester his first Ride & Tie finish.

The presence of unforeseen factors, however, does not mean that formulating a strategy is a wasted effort. Professional football players continue using carefully planned plays in spite of the fact that they rarely work exactly as planned. If they didn't continue, the likelihood of success would be more remote. Without a strategy, teammates would have no sense of coordination or timing. Without experimenting with strategies, a team would not be able to determine operational strengths and weaknesses. Without attempting the "perfect" play, you lose the potential opportunity of experiencing the perfect race. Another important reason for Ride & Tie strategies, even if they are spontaneous alternatives to an original plan, is to establish some measure of psychological security. Many Ride & Tie participants agree that not knowing where your teammates are or what they are doing is one of the worst feelings you can have. The resulting uncertainty and anxiety can be more tiring than the steepest hill. A plan to give you an idea of where the horse will be in relation to how long you have been running will encourage optimum performance. It will be easier to pace yourself if you know how far you have to run. If the horse isn't where it should be, having a strategy will at least let you know that something went wrong. With appropriate resolve, you can proceed as best you can, hoping that your partner can rectify whatever problem exists. In the 1973 Angels Camp (California) Ride & Tie, Jim Larimer continued running for twenty miles because he knew that his partner, Gordy Ainsleigh, was having trouble with the horse. He continued running because he had confidence in his partner's ability to adhere to their alternative game plan. With such mutual confidence and planning, they finished in second place.

The possibility of overpassing your horse can be minimized with a strategy. Although you must always look for your horse, knowing approximately where he will be tied is an important asset. It will allow you to focus more of your energy on running and less on searching. If the horse has, for example, stepped behind a tree, you have to make a concentrated effort to locate him when you are running. Knowing approximately when to make this effort will allow you to run more efficiently at other times. Remember, overrunning the horse is a common mistake in Ride & Tie. Any plan that will help minimize the risk is valuable.

Planning a Team Strategy

Although there are as many strategies as there are Ride & Tie teams, the following represent the most common ones. Whatever strategy you choose, however, it should include several basic components. It should take into consideration the individual capabilities of each team member. It should be responsible to the well-being of the horse at all times. (A horse will run itself to death if you ask it of him.) And, it should be based on spending as little time as possible at the Vet Checks.

One strategy alternative is based on mileage. This requires that each teammate be able to judge approximately how far he or she has travelled on horseback during a particular riding turn. For example, the plan could be to ride the horse two miles at a time. Or, if running capabilities are different, one rider could ride for two miles and the other could ride for three miles. One problem with this strategy is that it is sometimes possible to outrun the horse. If a section of the course is flat and downhill, a good runner might catch up to the horse and be forced to slow down if his mileage increment is almost ended. Another disadvantage is that the amount of work each runner has to perform may be inequitable on some courses. For example, a particular course may have an uphill climb about every two miles. This is another reason to adjust your strategy to a particular course.

Another alternative is to use "timed rides." Although this will require the use of watches, it will assure a more even distribution of the work load on some courses and will eliminate the need for estimating mileage. Also, the horse's pace and distance will be limited to the same extent as the runner's. Since time, not distance, is the determining factor, each runner will exert a relatively equal effort, regardless of the terrain. One runner may have to run one mile uphill, but the other runner will have to run twice as far downhill. By knowing how fast your horse can travel on various terrains, you can determine about how far you will have to run each time.

For this strategy to work effectively, timing should begin the moment the rider passes the runner and not when the horse is picked up at the tie. This will prevent the plan from being upset if the runner gets too far in front of the rider. For example, the rider may start the race and ride a chosen time of five minutes. After five minutes, he ties the horse and sets out on foot. In about eight minutes the runner who started on foot will arrive at the place where the horse is tied and begin riding. When he passes the runner, he yells out the time on his watch or the time it will be when he ties the horse, which should be exactly five minutes longer. For maximum efficiency, the runner should run slightly easier while waiting for his team to pass and faster when the five minute increment begins. This will help assure that runners do not outrun the horse so that it takes a long time for the rider to catch up to a leading runner. The condition of the horse is important in determining how long a timed increment should be. The shorter the time, the less time the horse will have to rest between changeovers. Thus, if a team's strategy is to keep close to each other, running short distances and communicating frequently, it is imperative that the horse be in sufficient condition to maintain a competitive pace without longer rest periods. On the other hand, too long a time increment could cause some problems for the runner, the rider, or the horse. Lengthy rests for the horse, for example, can cause his muscles to stiffen and can prevent him from running his most efficient race. The best way to determine the best increment for your team is to practice, observe, and compare during training.

Regardless of what strategy you are using, it must include the importance of the Vet Check. Ideally, you want to keep both human teammates moving. If one teammate is forced to wait at a checkpoint for his horse to be released, this forward progress is checked. This problem will most likely occur if the horse is brought in for a tie just ahead of the following runner. Strategies should be adjusted in such a way to assure that the horse will be brought into the checkpoint far enough ahead of the following runner to be able to rest sufficiently before it is examined by a veterinarian. If, for example, a rider is two minutes from his designated tie point, but only five minutes from the checkpoint, he should modify the strategy and continue into the checkpoint. Otherwise, the following man will have to bring the horse in and wait for him to recover from three minutes of riding. Knowing when to modify your strategy depends on knowing the locations of the Vet Checks. If you have not been able to preride the course completely, you should pay close attention to the map descriptions of landmarks and mileage. A well-organized race will have enough marshalls along the course to tell you how far ahead checkpoints are. If you have had an opportunity to learn the course, then you have an advantage. In fact, if you know the course very well, you can use another strategy alternative based on predesignated locations. With this strategy, you and your partner can choose specific places at which the horse will be tied all along the course. In preparing this plan, all aspects of timing, terrain, and individual capabilities can be considered.

Often, a preplan can include a mixture of timed riding increments and predesignated locations. This works well when there are stretches of terrain with no place to tie a horse. A preride of the course might uncover some hitching object slightly off the trail or before a barren stretch. Even if you were using a timed increment strategy, you might want to plan on using such an object to prevent too long a ride or run if the tie were missed. Also, there might be ideal tie spots outside of each Vet Check that you would want to designate as interruptions to otherwise timed rides. On courses where there are long stretches of terrain without hitching objects naturally available, a strategy might include the use of "living tie posts." Most Ride & Tie rules allow a team to have crewpersons stationed at specific areas to hold a team's horse. Such use of manpower can be very valuable in maintaining your strategy and keeping your forward progress going. Not only do you not have to worry about finding a place to tie, but "living posts" can carry water for you and the horse. Although this practice has been allowed in the National Ride & Tie, I am not convinced that it is a fair rule because many competitors, especially those who travel long distances to races, are not able to gather enough dedicated and energetic volunteers willing to hike to such areas.

Although having a specific game plan is recommended, some teams are expert enough to compete with a well-calculated "ad-lib." Such teams know the capabilities of all members of the team. They also have an intuitive and experienced awareness of what to do and when to do it based on diligent training and knowledge. If a rider knows an approaching hill will be long and steep and that he is the better uphill runner, he may want to tie the horse at the bottom of the hill even though he may have just passed his partner. If teammates have this confidence and consideration, spontaneous decisions can be successful throughout a race.

Although the flexibility, understanding, and confidence necessary to make this last strategy work should be inherent in every strategy, I wouldn't recommend such a loose plan unless you and your teammates have competed and practiced together for several years. Having a specific game plan, and being able to adjust it to the many variables that may occur, will provide for better coordination of effort during training and competition.

Tactics

Awareness of the tactics available during Ride & Tie can serve to increase your team's chances for success. Knowing how and when to take advantage of tactics adds an even greater sense of refinement and professionalism to Ride & Tie. Using certain tactics can, at times, protect the well-being of both yourself and the horse. At other times, they can give you a psychological advantage over an opponent. Although some tactics depend upon pregame planning and practice, many are merely a matter of common sense. But in Ride & Tie, even common sense sometimes requires a little forethought to be properly exercised.

Improving Team Performance

The "running changeover" is one tactic that can be used effectively. Regardless of what strategy is being used, there may be times when a runner will want to change to riding as soon as the horse and rider approach him. Perhaps he has been running too long. He may have a cramp or may have just finished a tough uphill. Depending on other variables, such as the condition of the horse or the rider, overall progress might be enhanced if the changeover is made before the planned tie point is reached. In order to prepare for this possible situation and save important seconds during the change, the rider should be alert for his running partner until he begins to approach him from the rear. When the rider is within hearing range, he should call out, "How are you doing?" to his partner. If the runner acknowledges a need to start riding, the change can be made with very little loss of forward momentum and the original strategy can be resumed as though the new rider had just picked the horse up from a tie. Since the horse will be going twice as far as usual without a rest, this tactic should be used only when necessary and only if the horse is in top condition.

Another important tactic that can be employed, if you think the horse and your team will benefit by it, is running alongside your horse. This tactic can be used on uphill grades especially, where your forward speed will not be greatly reduced and if you think your extra running effort will save the horse for a more important riding stretch later. It also can be used on steeper downhill slopes to protect the horse from the damaging concussion that can occur when riding him down at an equally fast pace. No time is lost because you usually will be able to run down a hill alongside your horse on foot as fast as you can ride him and with relatively little energy spent. The tactic of running alongside your horse can be useful on level terrain. If you see that your horse is beginning to tire, allowing him to run alongside you could be just the respite he needs to catch a second wind. It can prevent the possibility of injury or overwork later in the race. Or, it can prepare him for a tough uphill ride. Constant awareness of your horse's condi-

It is best to lead the horse over real rough terrain spots on the trail. (Scotty Ray Morris)

tion and getting the most out of him without overdoing it is good horsemanship in any situation. But in Ride & Tie good horsemanship is necessary to finish a race and should be used as a tactic to aid in optimal performance.

When uphill slopes are so steep that you cannot maintain a good forword speed on foot, but you are concerned with tiring your horse under your weight, the tactic of *tailing* (explained in the previous chapter) should be used. If you are in excellent condition you can tail a horse up a hill almost as fast as you can ride him. Be sure you are not so fatigued as to become "dead weight" on the horse's back when you mount at the top of the hill. The horse will be tired as well and if you do not ride him properly, your fatigue will transmit to the horse.

Running alongside your horse just before you stop to tie him is another good tactic in Ride & Tie. Making a sudden stop, rushing to tie the horse, and hurrying to start your foot-race can leave an already nervous animal even more nervous. Such nervousness can increase the possibility of the horse trying to pull away from the tie, injuring himself, or losing important rest time. Reducing his work effort prior to stopping him will also decrease the possibility of his muscles getting stiff or of blood pooling. Coming into a tie area on foot makes it easier for you to choose a convenient tie spot. Bringing a horse to a tie place at a more relaxed pace, calmly tying him, and quietly setting off on your run will not take much time and can prevent many problems.

Another tactic that will help maintain the good condition of your four-legged teammate is loosening the girth immediately after the tie. (This may not be necessary, however, if you are already riding with a very loose girth.) It allows the horse to breathe easier and thus recuperate faster. It is a good idea, after loosening the cinch, to throw the stirrup up over the saddle to remind your partner that the saddle is loose. Otherwise, he is apt to forget and find himself on the ground with the saddle hanging upside down under the horse's belly. It is easy to forget such things after an exhausting run when you are anxious to start riding for a while. It is also a good idea to have the rider adjust the stirrup length for the approaching runner.

Choosing the right place to tie the horse also can be an important tactic. If possible, it should be easy to unwrap the rope from around the object to which it is tied. Also, the horse should not be tied so short that it will be difficult to slack the rope enough to unsnap it. Nor should it be tied so long that the horse can trip himself, become entangled, or block the trail for other teams. Tying next to an embankment should be avoided to prevent either the horse or the approaching runner from losing his footing during the mount. The horse also should be tied so that he can be mounted without blocking the way of passing teams. And finally, the horse should not be tied so close to another horse as to provoke hostility or to get kicked by a strange horse.

Advantage over Opponents

Aside from tactics to increase the performance of your team, there are tactics to decrease the performance of your competitors. In an Oklahoma Ride & Tie, for example, the winning team used a tactic the owner of their horse uses regularly in fifty-mile endurance rides. The horse, apparently, was in excellent condition and the riders knew its capabilities. With this information in mind, a rider would "seduce" nearby competitors into a faster pace than they should be

This horse waits patiently, as trained, seemingly unaware of runners and horses passing beside him. (Scotty Ray Morris)

going. Keeping the horse at the brink of exertion, the opponent's horses become overworked and are forced to slow to a pace even slower than they were originally travelling. When this occurs, the seducing horse is brought back to a normal pace. This same tactic can be used in a footrace. If you think you are in good enough shape to outrun your nearest competitor for a short distance without putting yourself out of commission, you might be able to psych him into a secondary position. This tactic works well on steep hills. As you approach your opponent from behind, begin preparing yourself for a surge of effort. Try to use this tactic on a section of trail that is winding and hilly so that once you pass him you will be out of sight. In this way, you can slow down to rest in the blind spots and then continue running hard when you can be seen. If your opponent thinks you are going to keep up the blinding pace at which you passed him, it is likely that he may concede the front-running position and slow to a more sane pace.

Another tactic that has been used to psychologically discourage an opponent is simply talking to him. Although this won't work on everyone, some runners become seriously chagrined if they are running hard and someone alongside them is conversing freely. The best way to use this tactic is to approach an opponent from behind and begin a friendly conversation. (Stay behind the opponent so he will not see you working just as hard, if not harder, than he or she is.) Rather than talking, you may just want to start singing a song nonchalantly. (You will find that some songs are easier to sing during a vigorous run than others and, with practice during training, you will find one that can be sung without revealing labored breathing. I have found that "Home on the Range" works well.) After a short while, you will have psychologically worn your opponent down to a point where he will be glad you passed him.

I enjoy this tactic, whether it works on a competitor or not. The talking and singing help me control my breathing and take my mind off the effort of running. But although it is fun for me to do, it can be obnoxious to another runner. For example, in the Olema (California) Ride & Tie, I found myself running behind "Cowman" Ken Shirk. "Cowman," with his annual red, white, and blue beard, is a regular member of the Ride & Tie family and is as good a runner as he is colorful. We were running up a long hill and I was running directly behind him to take advantage of his excellent pacing and to use his large frame to block the wind resistance. As we struggled up the hill, I began talking about how beautiful the view of the Pacific Ocean was from our vantage point and how great it would be to be diving for abalone and drinking beer. Only once did the usually talkative "Cowman" answer and I could tell that he was tired of my talking. Within fifteen minutes, I came upon my horse and we were separated. About an hour later, however, our paths met again. I was rounding a turn and saw him tying his horse just ahead of me. He didn't see me and I resumed my position at his heels. After a while I continued the same conversation about abalone and beer, as though I had been following him all the time. This time, he turned his head in disbelief and said, "Hey, man, let's wait till after the race to talk!" At that, I began singing my "Abalone Song" and before I finished a chorus, I was able to pass him easily. I even remember the chorus:

> *Some live on hope*
> *And some on dope*
> *And some on matrimony.*
> *But I'm content*
> *To pay my rent*
> *And live on abalone!*

Two-time Levi's Ride & Tie champion Ken Williams used such a tactic in the Paso Robles Ride & Tie. Veteran Ride & Tie participant and top contender Jim Remillard commented on it to reporters after the race, won by Ken and his teammates Don Roth and "Pathfinder." "It's pretty deadly serious at the front in a race like this," Remillard said. "There were several of us in that thick manzanita where there wasn't room to pass when Williams caught up with us, laughing and complaining that we were going too slow. He was apparently having a good time when the rest of us were tense and I knew that we were in touble. Williams was going to be tough the rest of the way. I felt that he had a good chance to win."* Once a competitor concedes this to you, you have already scored a tactical victory. A little extra effort at pretending can often give you just enough of an edge to outdistance him.

Tactics can be used on the many narrow trails that are encountered in Ride & Tie. For example, if you are running on a narrow trail steep enough to keep a horse running at about the same speed as a human, it is best to try and stay ahead of the horses. This way, you will avoid losing the time and inconvenience of trying to get out of the way of a rider who wants to pass. (As a rider, every effort should be made to pass a runner safely. To assure a smooth passing action, you should be sure of your route and yell out the side on which you will be passing the runner. "Passing on the right, please" is a common exclamation during Ride & Tie competition.)

Usually, you will hear a horse approaching from behind before it gets close enough to attempt to pass and you can start to speed up. If the horse is gaining and the rider asks to pass, you should carefully and quickly choose a safe spot off the side of the trail and jump onto it. Be sure you do not jump off a cliff or into a tree, but remember that a clump of poison oak may be better than getting run over by a horse. If the situation is reversed and the runner desires to pass a slower moving horse, you should tell the rider that you intend to pass at the first possible opportunity. Otherwise, it may be better to fall back away from the dust and rocks kicked up by the horse.

* "Ride & Tie," *True Magazine,* December 1975, p. 52.

9
Vet Check

Make sure that you race
At an adequate pace
To bring your horse home feeling fine.
If you do as you should,
And treat your horse good,
He'll bring you to the finish line.

Following the fourth Levi's Ride & Tie in Klamath Falls, Oregon, Gordy Ainsleigh, a member of the winning team, was asked to explain what he thought was the most important aspect of Ride & Tie performance. His answer was, "to get the horse through the Vet Checks." There is no doubt that successful negotiation through each Vet Check is the most important factor in Ride & Tie. If your horse shows indications of being unable to endure the remainder of a rugged course, then the battle is lost. An overused, injured, or depressed animal will end your attempt to meet the challenge of Ride & Tie.

Purpose of Vet Checks

Ride & Tie events demand that veterinarian checkpoints be thorough in investigating the horse's health. There are usually three major Vet Checks and three "eyeball" checks during the competition. Ever since the accidental deaths of two horses in the first Ride & Tie competition, every effort has been made in the National Ride & Tie to assure that teams are allowed to continue only if their horses are fit. Since that first race, many distinguished veterinarians, including Jerry Gillespie, William Benthan, R. B. Barsaleau, Murray Fowler, Kerry Ridgeway, Jim Steere, and others, have researched equine physiology as it applies to the stresses of endurance racing. Furthermore, they have applied this research to Ride

& Tie to come up with safe and realistic standards of performance. Although specific standards may vary, depending on local weather, terrain, and the discretion of the veterinarians in charge, most Ride & Tie Vet Checks adhere to the guidelines discussed in this chapter.

The primary concern of Vet Checks in Ride & Tie are the pulse and respiration rates. A horse is usually not considered ready to continue until his pulse and respiration are both seventy actions per minute. Nor will a horse be allowed to leave a checkpoint if the respiratory rate is higher than the pulse rate, even if the rates are lower than seventy. The horse will be checked for an exhaustion syndrome that causes abnormal contractions of the heart and diaphragm, as indicated by a "thumping" in the chest wall. Other irregularities in heart function that may be revealed by a stethoscope can also be judged as disqualifying by the veterinarian. Other disqualifying factors include injuries that may have been sustained on the trail such as puncture wounds, serious abrasions, cuts, or avulsions. Any sign of lameness, whether from a stone bruise, a sore tendon, or a pulled muscle, will be justification to withdraw a horse from the competition. Muscle stiffness, indicating the tying up syndrome or sore joints, can be disqualifying. The veterinarians also check for signs of exhaustion, including a relaxed anal sphincter, a temperature over 103 degrees, obvious depression indicated by a disinterest in various stimuli, or an unwillingness to move. The areas where tack can cause sore spots are checked. Intestinal noise is observed to assure there is adequate circulation and muscular movement of the digestive tract. And finally, the resiliency of the skin is tested to see if the horse is overly dehydrated.

Examination of the horse is even more complete during the preride Vet Check than it is in the mid-route checks. At this check, held the day before the race, more time can be spent assuring that the horse is ready for Ride & Tie. Disqualifying factors include any detectable lameness, sore muscles, swollen tendons, damaged or cracked hooves, or improper shoeing. If shoeing can be corrected, the vet can order that it be done before he will pass your horse. A veterinarian can disqualify a horse if he thinks there is a lack of adequate muscle tone or if the horse is overly fat.

At the preride check, mucous membranes and nasal passages are checked for color and excessive discharge. Internal sounds are carefully monitored to determine cardio-respiratory irregularities. Pulse and respiration rates are recorded and, although allowance is usually made for excitability, excessive rates can cause disqualification. Saddle sores, cuts, and scars will be noted and those deemed serious enough can also disqualify the horse.

It is during the preride Vet Check that the veterinarians assure themselves that the horse is at least five years of age and not pregnant. They are concerned with the possibility of finding a drugged horse or one that has recently recovered from an illness or colic. They also determine if the disposition of the horse is adequate for competition. An animal that has potentially dangerous tendencies, such as kicking or rearing, can hurt himself and other participants.

You and your partner must do everything possible to maintain the good condition of your horse during both training and competition. Proper strategy will help assure that the horse has time to recuperate from a hard ride before he is brought to a veterinarian for inspection. However, no matter how conscientious your effort, assuming you are riding competitively, your horse's recovery can be enhanced with proper care at the Vet Checks. In order to insure such care is provided, your Ride & Tie preparations should include finding and training a pit crew.

Use of a Pit Crew

Members of a Ride & Tie pit crew are the unsung heroes of the event. A good pit crew can mean the difference between survival and defeat. Not only will crewpersons be invaluable in helping your horse recover rapidly, but they can help to keep the human element of the team in good shape. In the Olema Ride & Tie, I might not have been able to continue the race in good form if it weren't for the massage, refreshments, and moral support furnished by my wife, the Lantis family, and other members of our pit crew. Owing to an injury suffered by my partner, I was, at one point, obliged to run further than I was prepared to run. Furthermore, because of our good position in the race, I pushed myself too hard for the distance I had to run. I started the run from the twenty-four-mile checkpoint and was the very first runner to leave. The enthusiasm of knowing I was running in first place quickened my pace even more. After a couple of miles, however, I began to worry about my teammates and began looking over my shoulder for them. Then, Tom Laris passed me like I was standing still. As I watched him disappear ahead of me, his teammate, Ken Williams, came riding past me on horseback. Depression hit me. My legs started to feel like sponges and their ability to move seemed to come only from the lift of my shoulders. Two more teams passed me before my teammates finally arrived, less than a mile from the next checkpoint. I knew that our horse would need rest, so I motioned to my partner to continue to the checkpoint and give the horse to our pit crew.

"I'm hurting pretty bad," he spoke as he rode past. "I got knocked down by a horse."

"Then we'll just survive to the finish," I yelled. "Let's just survive!"

But at that point, it seemed that our survival was dependent on our pit crew. Without them, my partner might not even have been able to dismount. They literally had to lift him off the horse. Then, within a few moments, they massaged, sponged, cooled, and nourished him. When they sent him on his way they turned their attention to the horse. By the time I arrived, my legs were literally ready to collapse. While half of my crew worked on the horse, the others massaged my legs and fed me electrolytes, glucose, and water. By the time the horse was ready, I had regained my strength and was ready to face the final ten-mile stretch to the finish. Without our pit crew, we never would have been able to maintain our fifth-place position to the finish line. As I left the checkpoint, I felt moved by the warmth, concern, team spirit, and camaraderie displayed by the pit crew.

The emotional impact of crewing a Ride & Tie is probably greater than that experienced by the runners. Families, horse owners, and friends stand by, frantically anticipating the arrival of a rider or runner. They know the outcome of the race may be in their hands. Many crewmembers have planned and trained for the Ride & Tie as long as the competing team. Chuck Stalley of Chico, California, and his crew have been working together since he originated the concept of a pit crew at the 1972 Levi's Ride & Tie. His horse for that race was named Peanuts and his crew wore T-shirts imprinted with the slogan, "I work for Peanuts." The fact that his team won may have been responsible for the pit crew becoming an integral part of Ride & Tie competition.

The first priority of a pit crew is to determine the location of the major Vet Checks and plan how teammates will get there. It is only necessary to have crewpersons at the major Vet Checks, where examinations include pulse and respiration recovery. (Although it is grand to have crew located along the entire course, most teams do not have the manpower.) Ideally, you should have enough trained people to station each Vet Check with a different group. It is more than likely, however, that you will just have one group moving from one checkpoint to another. Since course distances range over thirty to forty miles of rugged terrain, the logistics of placing your crew, equipment, and water can be difficult. Where vehicles are not allowed, it may be necessary for your crew to ride or hike to locations. Carrying gear up and down the trails and rushing from one checkpoint to another will sometimes require a well-conditioned crew. For this reason, you should start your friends and family on their own running program early in the year. Training to be a pit crew member can be a fun and rewarding way to physical fitness.

Once a crew has planned how it will reach the checkpoints at the required time, they should make sure they have all the necessary equipment. Such equipment should include a water bucket (with water if it is not available at the checkpoint), a blanket or cooler, a grooming brush, a hoof pick, a leather punch and string for tack repairs, electrolytes, and a first-aid kit for both the runners and the horse. If the checkpoint is conveniently located and can be reached by car, the pit crew will probably want to pack food and refreshments for everyone. Some hay can be brought for the horse to take

The team's pit crew is readying the horse for a major Vet Check.
(Scotty Ray Morris)

his mind off all the excitement. Green grass, if available, is preferable; but he should not eat too much. (Under no circumstance should he eat grain.)

When a horse arrives at one of the mid-route Vet Checks and the rider sets off on foot, the pit crew should immediately loosen the girth and begin walking the horse at a slow pace. A well-conditioned horse can recover better at a slow walk than when standing still. Walking him will keep his circulation adequate and will help prevent stiff muscles. While the horse is being walked, the saddle can be lifted slightly to allow fresh air to circulate under the pad. The saddle shouldn't be removed or pressure bumps might occur resulting from blood rushing to where the warm weight of the saddle has been.

The slow walking of the horse should be interrupted to cool him down and allow him to drink. After he is sponged and watered, he should be walked more and the process repeated until the horse is fully recovered. When cooling the horse it is best to use tepid water. Leaving a bucket of water in the sun will usually do the job. During the first cooling, the legs of the horse from the knees down should be sponged liberally. It is not a good idea to put water, especially cold water, directly on the horse's major muscle groups while he is still very hot. The effect will not be relaxing and can delay lowering the pulse rate. It also could cause cardiac irregularity. After another moment of walking, allow him to drink as much water as he desires. If he is accustomed to the taste of electrolytes in his water, it is usually a good idea to add a very small amount. Otherwise, don't risk his not drinking the water by adding anything. After he has been allowed to drink, you should sponge his head, ears, neck, and lower legs again.

Preparing for Final Inspection

If, at this point, the horse is still not ready to be presented for inspection, his bridle (if you are using one) should be removed and he should be allowed to nibble on grass or hay until he settles down. If the horse is not interested in eating, the crew should continue walking and sponging him. If the horse is brought before a veterinarian and he is not passed, ten minutes must elapse before he can be brought back for another inspection. Ride & Tie rules require that a member of the team present the horse, so the final responsibility for assuring that he has recovered fully is up to you. The pit crew, however, should be equally proficient in taking the horse's pulse and respiration to assure that everything is being done to make him ready by the time you or your partner arrive at the checkpoint.

Preparing your horse for his final inspection reminds you that you are a partner to him, not just a passenger. In monitoring his recovery, you are reminded of the many physiological and psychological similarities between the two of you. The use of massage and yoga-type movements at a Vet Check illustrates another similarity. If stretching and massage can rejuvenate your own stiff, aching, and tired muscles after a long run, it stands to reason that the muscles of the horse could benefit as well. This is especially true during preparation for a recovery check. The use of yoga movements and massage on our horse was one of the reasons he managed to pass through every Vet Check without delay in his first Ride & Tie competition.

Applying the principles of massage and yoga to the horse has been promoted by Dr. James Steere. It was his participation in Ride & Tie that prompted him to study the idea. Although Steere has a long list of distinguished credentials, it was his experience as a Ride & Tie competitor that made him realize the benefits of acupuncture, acupressure, massage, and yoga on endurance horses. As a beginning distance runner, he first explained the effects of stretching and massage on his own fatigued, shortened muscles, and stiff, aching joints. Understanding the similarity between man and animal after his first Ride & Tie, he applied the same successful principles on the horse. After five years of practice and observation, he is now convinced that having a pit crew massage the major working muscles of the horse for five or more minutes can improve the horse's recovery rate. Furthermore, stretching the horse's legs with yoga-type movements has shown to improve the performance of the horse after a stop at a Vet Check. In order to use the techniques effectively during a Vet Check, they should be practiced often during training. The horse should be comfortably accustomed to having his muscles stretched and massaged, and the pit crew should be accustomed to working with the horse in this way. When the horse is massaged, the large muscles should be worked with the fist or the edge of the palm. The legs should be massaged between the thumb and fingers. When stretching the legs of the horse, it is important to do each exercise slowly and gently. Try to stimulate every natural movement the horse is capable of performing and gently stretch his legs through the movement to a slightly abnormal range of motion. Hold each position for about ten seconds just as though you were stretching your own muscles. Stretching and massage should be done daily during training. In fact, stretching exercises before and after workouts will provide the same immediate benefits they do for you before and after your runs.

One final note regarding successful preparation for the Vet Checks has to do with showmanship. In Ride & Tie, the fate of a team is very much in the hands of a particular veterinarian. Since subjectivity and objectivity are inseparable in human nature, it may be worthwhile to put some effort into the subjective aspect of the veterinarian's examination, starting with the important preride Vet Check. First of all, the horse should be well groomed. Often a well-groomed horse will not be examined quite as critically as an ill-kept horse. For example, your horse may have some minor swelling of the tendon that, in fact, would not inhibit his safe performance. If your horse were well groomed, a veterinarian would be more likely to agree with you, whereas if he looked unkempt, the vet might decide you have not been very careful with the horse and disqualify him.

It is also a good idea to keep your horse relatively quiet and well mannered at the preride Vet Check. If you allow

Horses should be calm and relaxed before being brought into a Vet Check area. Excited horses often cause panic with spectators, participants, and other horses, and can make a negative impression on the attending vet. (Jim Keane)

him to prance and strut about too much, he will look worse when he is tired during a mid-course Vet Check. If you can keep the horse calm during the preliminary check, try to make sure the examining official remembers you and the horse. Then, if you make sure the same official checks the horse mid-route, the horse will not seem to him to have lost as much energy and enthusiasm. Also, it might help for you to look energetic. A good veterinarian knows that a tired rider will make for a tired horse and this factor could enter into his decision.

And finally, it always pays to be courteous. No matter how anxious you may be to get out of a Vet Check, realize that the veterinarians are working as fast as they can. Making the examining official angry may be a sure way to lose ten minutes time if your horse is borderline. Such attitudes are not in keeping with the spirit of sportsmanship in Ride & Tie.

Part Four
Ride & Tie: The Event

10
Race Time

You've waited one year.
Now the moment is here.
The tension is mounting inside.
With the signal to start,
You call on your heart
For stamina, courage, and pride.

The days surrounding a Ride & Tie are as full of spirit and excitement as the race itself. In fact, it often seems as though the four or five hours of actual competition are but a temporary interruption to a continuous cycle of planning and preparation. The actual race serves as a highlight to a love affair more enduring than the challenging test it provides. Even the post-race ceremonies serve mainly to stimulate our urge to begin preparing for the next year's event. Nor is glory alone the incentive for this urge. More importantly, it comes from a desire to once again experience the unique blending of tranquility and celebration—the aftermath of Ride & Tie. This, combined with having another opportunity to express your full potential, is why very few Ride & Tie participants fail to return to the experience time and time again.

Arriving at a Race Site

For most people, race time begins the moment they arrive at the scene of the event with their horses, running shoes, and sleeping bags. Teams living within several hundred miles of the race site usually begin checking out the course on pre-rides about four weeks before race day, assuming the course has already been announced. These teams usually spend the weekends running and riding over the course. Within two weeks of the race day, the race site campgrounds begin filling with campers, cars, and horse trailers from all around the country.

By the time the last few days arrive, the campground is full of tents, trailers, horses, and people. The atmosphere is filled with laughter, music, Ride & Tie stories, comments about the difficulty of the course, and wagering on possible completion times. The aroma of the campground is typically western. The smell of horses, timothy hay, and barbecue blend with the fresh country air reminiscent of one's first county fair or rodeo. Even without the sounds and smells, there is an unmistakable air of excitement pervading the entire campground. Horses dance about nervously and people jog between campsights to release nervous energy.

Invariably, prerace events include a carbohydrate-loading party at the campsight of one of the local participant's homes. At the 1977 Olema Ride & Tie, my partner and I threw a kink in many diets by providing fresh abalone from the nearby Pacific Ocean. Everyone is welcome at such parties and newcomers are often amazed at the hospitality, warmth, and carefree attitudes put forth so close to the beginning of the race. Everyone is intoxicated by the spirit of camaraderie and excitement. At one party, with less than a glass of wine in my system, I began playing an accordian from atop my van while my partner drove it around the campfire. As we drove back to our campsight, I could be heard singing:

> *Two people and one horse*
> *Is all it takes.*
> *Some skill, some sweat, and some lucky breaks.*
> *You'll see grand land, with hills and lakes.*
> *And you'll do just fine if you don't see snakes!*
> *Ride & Tie, Ride & Tie*
> *We're gonna Ride & Tie, until the cows come*
> *   home.*

Social frivolity, however, does not get in the way of essential race time activities for most serious competitors. Learning the course is the major reason for arriving days before the actual race. Horses perform better when they are familiar with the terrain. Strategies can be planned, based on the location of hills and Vet Checks. Drinks can be stashed along the course. But most importantly, participants can minimize the possibility and worry of getting lost. In spite of attempts to assure the trails are well marked, every National Ride & Tie has seen at least one team get lost temporarily. People concentrate so much on their running, they sometimes fail to take the correct turn. The consequences are not always significant when a team member gets lost, but they are always alarming and frustrating. In 1971, Jim Larimer and Hal Hall were leading the race about seventeen miles from the start when they both got lost after missing the same turn. After about a mile, they showed up at a ranch house not having seen a race marker for some time. They knocked on the door and an old man appeared. When they asked if he knew the Ride & Tie trail, he answered by leading them to the junction in a 1948 pickup. Although they managed to win the race, the experience was nonetheless a harrowing one.

Many participants avoid getting lost during the race by getting lost during the preride instead. Paso Robles Ride & Tie winners Ken Williams and Don Roth became "hopelessly lost" during the second preride of that course. In the Northstar race, seventh-place finishers Norm Kreuter and Gino Pomilla set up camp three weeks before the day of the race. Their first day out, the two runners became separated on the trail. In an attempt to find each other, they became lost. As the sun began to set, their thoughts started to focus more on surviving the cold evening or getting back to camp alone. Their mutual search was abandoned and they both managed to find their way back to the campsite. They were not about to lose the course again, especially during the race.

Losing the way on a Ride & Tie course is not a matter of poor sense of direction. Such is the nature of the wilderness. One evening, several days before the 1977 Levi's Ride & Tie, news started around camp that Walt Stack and Hugh Bryson had not yet returned from a preride that had started at eleven o'clock in the morning. Stack and Bryson had been friends as labor radicals, and shipmates for many years. They were now united to meet the challenge of Ride & Tie. Hugh, president of the National Motel Association, and an experienced horseman, had just started running several months before the race. Walt, a hod carrier and marathon runner, had just started horseback riding. By nine o'clock, the camp

Walt Stack and Hugh Bryson walk their partner after winning the "Centurian in the Saddle" award at the 1977 Olema Ride & Tie. (Scotty Ray Morris)

started worrying about them. Just before a search party was organized, however, the two staggered into camp, with Walt on foot and Hugh on horseback. After eleven hours on the trail, the two looked healthy. However, all the usually talkative Stack had to say was, "We got lost."

Much of the prerace competitive spirit around the campsite is demonstrated by pit crews who begin showing up toward the end of the last week before race day. Walt Schafer of Chico, California, speaks of the spirit of common adventure and encouragement evident among the members of the pit crews. Schafer had twenty-five friends from his hometown crewing for him in the 1977 Levi's Ride & Tie. In an earlier event, Alan Jackson's pit crew, though smaller in number, was equal in motivation. They placed a large sign in their camp reading,

"Remember, Peanuts is training!" The sign referred to the horse of "the team to beat" that year and was reminiscent of a sign Jackson's friends used when he was training for the 1961 International Pentathlon in the Soviet Union. That sign read, "Remember, the Russians are training."

Pre-Race Activities

By the time race day eve arrives, the planning and partying stage of prerace activities is over. The runners have settled into a forced state of relaxation and the campground takes on the feel of a calm before the storm. Only by observing the horses can one get the true pulse rate of the camp. The relative inactivity is, however, interrupted, not only by the nervous horses, but also by individuals looking for new horses to replace horses disqualified at the preride Vet Check. Levels of disappointment vary among these individuals but all seem to take it in stride. They know the decision was for the good of the horse and that such disappointments are part of the Ride & Tie game. Last-minute hopes of finding a horse or teammate are not unusual the day before the race. Joyce Spearman and Marty Ginsburg were two teammates who were "praying for a horse" so they would have an opportunity to try and beat the six-time women's division champions, Dawn Damas and Mary Tiscornia. Others have horses available but no partner. Dianne Ripley of Auburn, California, waited until the last minute for her partner to arrive from Buenos Aires, Argentina, for the 1977 Levi's race. Fortunately, her partner, Carlos Ariju, a top-ranked polo player, showed up just in time. Having a teammate that lives so far away, however, does not always work out. Martha and Peter Klopfer, of Durham, North Carolina, rented their four-legged teammate from a trainer in Reno, Nevada, for the 1977 Olema race. Unfortunately, although the horse showed up, the animal was pulled at the first Vet Check. Peter, a professor of biology, and Martha, the mother of three and a champion marathon runner, had entered their first Ride & Tie in 1975 to celebrate their twentieth wedding anniversary. They won the Man-Woman team trophy that year and again in 1976. Having travelled so far to be the first three-time Man-Woman division champions in the history of the race, they were disappointed when their horse was pulled. However, their spirits remained high throughout the proceedings, although they were unable to find another horse. When asked about their disappointment they simply responded, "There's always next year."

Considering the itineraries of typical Ride & Tie participants, it is amazing there are not more last-minute cancella-
tions. For example, one participant, plastic surgeon John
Emery, was in the middle of opening a new medical clinic,
and not only managed to compete in the 1977 Levi's race, but
trained sufficiently to place in the top ten. There are also competitors like Barbara Magid, a schoolteacher raising two children, or teammates Rick Sylvester and Ron Nehring. Rick
teamed up with a partner who lived 1,000 miles away.
Furthermore, Ron, who had just completed the Boston
Marathon in 2:30, had to interrupt preparations for his law
school exam to fly out for the race. The examples could go
on through the entire list of Ride & Tie participants, from
self-employed business people to factory workers. In spite of
their schedules, they manage to find time for Ride & Tie.

Perhaps one reason teams are able to hold together as well
as they do has to do with the dedication of their horse sponsors. The people who furnish and train horses for teams are as
concerned about the race as the team itself. Although these
people are usually professional horse trainers, their dedication in providing a horse for a team goes far beyond the
limits of their jobs. Often, they also serve as riding instructors,
strategists, or in pit crews. The horse sponsors for Ride & Tie
teams are usually as exciting and colorful as the participants
themselves. One such person is Virl O. Norton, winner of the
Great American Horse Race across the United States. In a
letter written to me by Adrian Vandenhoogen and his son Ed, a
team whose animal was sponsored by Norton in a Ride & Tie,
the characteristics of Norton were described. The letter,
entitled, "A Mule Man with a Big Heart," explained that two
days before the race the Vandenhoogen's horse came up
lame. Ed had crewed endurance races for Norton and knew
that he had a soft spot for kids. He asked if Norton could be
of help and without delay the team was offered Virl's cross-
country race-winning mule, Lady Louise. Knowing that the
inexperienced team would not be "in the money," Virl still
personally delivered the high-priced animal and pit crewed
for the price of a thank you and the satisfaction of seeing
twelve-year-old Ed achieve his first National Ride & Tie
completion buckle.

Bill Davis is another horse trainer who dedicates himself to providing top quality horses for Ride & Tie teams. Davis goes all out, both as a horse trainer and as a team coach, and is the kind of coach who commands respect. Davis, who in the thirties, made his living capturing alligators and rattlesnakes, once demonstrated how much trust he had in his horse, Pathfinder, by lifting the 900-pound Arabian off the ground. When such a man loans you a horse, you are not likely to come up empty-handed on race day. Furthermore, it is not likely that you will intentionally disappoint the kind of a sponsor who, like Bill Davis, has finished a fifty-mile endurance ride after setting his own broken leg at the start.

The list of sponsors and a description of their colorful backgrounds would be as interesting as a description of the competitors themselves. What is important, however, is that people like Virl Norton, Bill Davis, Cliff Lewis, John Kostelic, and others are partly responsible for the high percentage of teams who make it to the starting line each year. The fact that most of these people are uniquely talented, interesting, and dedicated themselves, simply confirms the Ride and Tie spirit.

The Starting Line-Up

The long lines at the campground bathroom facilities early in the morning is a sure sign that race day has arrived. Throughout the camp, horses are being trotted out. If you will be a starting rider, it is a good idea to bring the horse to the designated starting point and ride the course for about a quarter-mile. This should be done about one-half hour before the start. Ideally, you should make this trip several times so that your last trip back is just in time for the real start. This will accomplish several things. First, it will assure that your horse is adequately warmed up. Second, the horse will be more likely to follow the desired route in spite of the confusion and excitement of the start. The immediate familiarity with the route will tend to prevent him from following another horse. And third, the procedure will help minimize the amount of nervous tension accumulated while waiting for the starting signal. Nervous tension preceding athletic competition is a common phenomenon. The "butterflies," the rapid heart rate, the active bowels, and the emotional extremes are all indications that sports are stimulating. The excitement of the countdown before a Ride & Tie start is also the moment true bonding of teammates occurs. The energy emitted from the horse becomes inseparable from that of the rider. Last minute handshakes and well-wishes confirm the fact that the race is against the elements, not one another.

As the countdown approaches the one-minute mark, the realization that the race is actually starting finally takes hold. Tears seem to swell up uncontrollably. One man on your left starts to cry out loud. You recognize him as being the winner of a previous Ride & Tie in which he finished the race with a lacerated scalp and a bleeding tailbone. You remember him as a man who showed no emotion over the pain. To your right, a girl is struggling to keep control of her horse. She also has been crying, although she seems angry at herself for it. It is her first Ride & Tie and she cannot understand why her horse is acting differently than before. When the countdown reaches thirty seconds, you realize you also feel compelled to cry out. Just before you do, however, one of the riders yells, "When are they going to let that damn fox go?" The humor confuses your emotions and before you have time to respond, the race has begun.

A 1972 *Runner's World* article by Steve Murdock described the start of a Ride & Tie as looking like a "guerrilla cavalry charge supported by irregular infantry." In the Northstar Ride & Tie, two riders fell off their horses and one runner was run over before they had gone a hundred yards. This does not occur too often, but it is a good reminder that you should be extremely careful at the start. Although every effort is made to control the horses, the excitement and adrenaline of the moment make it difficult. The best rule if you are running is to start out slow and let the horses all get ahead of you. If you are riding and cannot slow or turn your horse, be sure to yell a warning to runners who may be in your path.

The drama that occurs in a Ride & Tie event, once it is underway, is unique for each person regardless of position in

At the beginning of competition, let the horses get out in front. (Scotty Ray Morris)

the race. Each individual is testing himself to his limits and will experience a unique set of circumstances along the way. For some individuals, like Olympian Tom Laris, the test is measured by the team's proximity to a first-place finish. Tom tried for four years to place near the top. In 1976, he almost made seventh place, but his partner tied the horse unexpectedly near the end of the race and Tom sprinted past the horse to the finish line. By the time the horse was retrieved, they were in eleventh place. Finally, in 1977, Tom achieved his mark. After once having admitted that his running career had existed only because he was "good at it" and that running was more work than fun for him, I asked him if he would try it again, now that he had won. "Well," he said, "I *am* starting to enjoy riding now." Another participant for whom a first-place finish became a major goal was Dick Fonseca, a forty-two-year-old insurance broker from Van Nuys, California. Dick has been a contender in the Ride & Tie since 1974, when he and his teammate ran eight miles in the wrong direction and then backtracked for a total of sixteen extra miles. In the 1975 race, he missed second place (and $1,837) by only five seconds. In 1976, he once again took third place. By the 1977 race, he was determined to reach his goal, and had been training 118 miles a week in preparation. His competitive determination, however, did not overshadow his more genuine Ride & Tie spirit. At one point along the trail my partner, who had been run over by a horse, was having trouble mounting our horse. As he was struggling, Fonseca, who was racing past, stopped to help. That year his team took seventh place and our team took fifth.

Such consideration among Ride & Tie competitors is common on the wilderness trails during a race. In one race, a rider had lost control of his horse and was beginning to panic as it approached a downhill incline. Another man, riding alongside, could be seen yelling out instructions and cautioning the first rider to relax. His yelling saved the rider from being knocked off the horse by a low branch. In another case, one competitor stayed with another, who had taken a bad fall, until medical aid arrived almost an hour later. This concern over fellow competitors seems intrinsic regardless of their sense of competition. In Point Reyes, California, Mark Driscoll and I were racing neck and neck halfway through the race, when I took a wrong turn. It would have been easy for him to let me continue, but instead he yelled at me to turn back.

The fact that Ride & Tie is basically a defensive game encourages this spirit. This is why such a diverse assortment of people can be competitive with one another. The outcome of the race has more to do with a team defending itself against the challenging variables than talent or aggressive athletics. Once again, the analogy between the concept of survival and Ride & Tie is touched upon. As in survival, the outcome depends on one's preparation, courage, determination, skill, and stamina in overcoming the elements; not on the defeat of

Gordon Ainsleigh and Ken Shirk sprint to the finish hand-in-hand at the 1977 Northstar Ride & Tie. Gordy and Ken are almost constant partners, and winners, in Ride & Tie. (Scotty Ray Morris)

an opponent. Since planning, ability, courage, determination, skill, and stamina are all characteristics equally attributable to both men and women, Ride & Tie is also the ultimate game for women. In the Olema Ride & Tie, 40 percent of the teams entered included women. Of the forty mixed and all-women teams, thirty-one finished the race compared to forty-seven out of sixty all-men teams. Two women, Carrie Walters and Marty Jensen, of Portland, Oregon, were on mixed teams that placed in the top ten. Although an all-woman team has never placed in the top ten of a National Ride & Tie, the long-distance running and riding capabilities of women make it possible.

Crossing the Finish Line

The finish of a Ride & Tie, although not as spectacular as the start, is equally exciting. By the end, the race has become a combination of races. The struggle for fiftieth place can be as exciting and as intense as the struggle for first place. Even if a participant is approaching the finish line unchallenged by another team, the crowd's response to his or her final effort is as enthusiastic as if the person were winning an Olympic gold medal. Mary Alice Kellogg, a San Francisco correspondent for *Newsweek,* attempted an in-the-field coverage of a Ride & Tie by entering a Levi's race. Dropping out after five miles, she stood at the finish line and watched. "The experience," she said, "left me envious of those panting people running, walking, tripping over the finish line."

Although the finish of a Ride & Tie sometimes looks like a slow-motion crawl to the last water hole, the pace often times picks up on the final stretch. Sometimes it happens when two teams are vying for the lead, and sometimes it is just to impress the crowd. Sometimes your pace quickens with the thrill of knowing you are finished. At any rate, the condition of the body at the end of a Ride & Tie is such that care should be taken not to overdo it. Several times runners have collapsed at the finish line. And some riders ask too much of their horses in the final effort of a race. Although most horse injuries occur early in a race, the increases in adrenaline and excitement that occur at the finish can excite the horse and cause his fatigued legs to stumble more easily.

On the last downhill in the 1977 Levi's Ride & Tie, Butch Alexander, three-time winner of the Ride & Tie, took a bad fall racing for fifth place and had to be taken to the hospital. Fortunately, his injuries were minor, but the incident shows that even an experienced competitor should be aware of this hazard. A good rule is to bring your horse into the finish as if he had another ten miles to go.

After you have finished and have been saturated with congratulations, there is a brief moment of reunion in the embrace of your partner. All the months of training and planning flash before you. As you embrace, the crowd, for a moment, seems isolated and unreal. Only you and your partner really understand what has transpired. Without this person you might have stopped or slowed down somewhere along the trail in pain or self-pity. But the thought that somewhere up ahead your teammate was working to his limit for your team forced you to keep going. As fellow competitors begin to cross the finish line, this drama repeats itself. Each individual has challenged and survived the race. No handshake is as important as that from a fellow competitor.

Camaraderie and sportsmanship, win or lose, are part of the spirit of Ride & Tie. (Matt Silverman)

Dr. Jim Steere, head veterinarian, and Bud Johns, originator of Ride & Tie, officiate over most Levi's Ride & Tie awards ceremonies. (Scotty Ray Morris)

Within an hour after the last team finishes, the chow lines begin to form as the aroma of barbeque chicken pervades the air. Soon after, a band starts playing music and couples begin kicking up their heels on the earthen dance floor. "After a day of racing up and down the mountains, they seem determined to stomp those mountains flat."* Once a group of runners has started dancing, the competitive spirit of tired runners sitting on the sidelines starts to rekindle and the number of dancers increases. Fortunately, before someone succumbs from exhaustion, the dancing is soon interrupted by the awards ceremony. It is during the awards presentation that "Ride & Tie fever" spreads. Teams who didn't finish are reminded of the glory of finishing as completion buckles are awarded. They begin assessing what went wrong and start making resolutions for the next year's ride. When the "In the Family" awards are given out, competitors and noncompetitors alike start thinking about how grand it would be if they could get their wife, husband, son, or daughter to train for, and win, such an award. What father could avoid being envious of the expressions on the faces of a team like Pat and twelve-year-old Donnie Browning as they received their first place "father-son" award in the 1977 National Ride & Tie?

* From *What Is This Madness,* a 1976 film about Ride & Tie, produced by Levi Strauss & Company.

What person in the audience, when watching Al and Marty Jensen or Peter and Martha Klopfer win an husband-wife award, didn't secretly imagine sharing such an experience with his or her mate?

The fever spreads as the awards continue. Two-women teams, especially, succumb when Dawn Damas and Mary Tiscornia time and again win the "Two-Women" team trophy. (Their 1977 win was their sixth Ride & Tie victory.) When the first-place trophy and money are awarded, the fever hits competitors who think they had a chance and could do better the next year. Plans for new training procedures or different horses begin to come into focus. Thoughts about new partners sneak into one's thoughts. The fever increases and spreads throughout the ceremony, from the presentation of completion buckles to the award for the best-conditioned horse. Everyone wants to improve his performance, and the anxiety to get started again takes hold.

After the awards ceremony, the party rapidly breaks up. People start preparing for their trip home or settle into their

Mary Tiscornia and Dawn Damas, six-time women's division champions, sprint toward the finish line. Mary and Dawn have dominated the women's division since their first attempt at the sport. (Matt Silverman)

tents to rest for an early morning departure. I remember leaving a postrace party and passing by my four-legged team-mate as he stood alone in a rope corral next to my van. The sun was setting and the noise of the band was muffled in the background. As I looked at the horse, who had done so well for us during the race, I felt a sense of guilt. He had been all but forgotten. He did not get a share of the prize money or an award. All the days of training we spent together flashed before me—the work, the worry, the excitement, the disappointment, the anger, and the satisfaction. The horse had been a part of it all. And now, almost choked with emotion, I found myself thanking him at last for a good job.

The horse, however, responded indifferently. He was sore and tired, but he was enjoying his hay and rest. He neither thought of the race gone by, nor the one to come. He had no plan or purpose. He had performed what he was capable of performing—no more, no less.

11
Organizing a Race

Consideration of knowledge returns a profit
Only after it is invested into action.
The value of action, however, is dependent
Upon planning, foresight, and effort.

The sport of Ride & Tie has gained both national and international attention since its invention in 1971. It is, however, still in its infancy and, next to the Levi's National Ride & Tie, there are only about a dozen other races annually organized. The need, therefore, is to increase the number of local Ride & Tie events around the country. Developing a Ride & Tie in your area can be an excellent opportunity for a community to experience the benefits and pleasures of such a game. Furthermore, the winning team in a local, sanctioned Ride & Tie will have its entry fee to the Levi's National Ride & Tie paid for by Levi Strauss & Company.

Committee Personnel

The first step in organizing a Ride & Tie is to appoint or hire a race manager. The race manager will then appoint, or hire, and supervise a group of individuals responsible for handling the various aspects of the event. This group can be referred to as the race committee, and the success of a Ride & Tie event depends almost entirely upon the committee. Members should include a treasurer, ride secretary, food chairman, head veterinarian, trail chairman, base camp manager, ride personnel manager, awards chairman, and publicity chairman.*

The responsibility of the treasurer includes opening a two-signature checking account specifically for the event. This account can be used for various expenses and for depositing

* See "Endurance Ride Manual," available from the California State Horsemen's Association, 897 Third Street, Santa Rosa, California.

the entry fees. The treasurer should also provide a comprehensive financial report for the race manager.

Ride Secretary. The ride secretary should be in charge of typing and mailing applications, maintaining a list of entries, and checking on specific permits that may be necessary (local authorities, humane society, state park, etc). The secretary will also prepare "Release of Responsibility" forms and assure that all participants have signed them. The secretary should also prepare race packets for participants that include rules and regulations, maps, race numbers, meal tickets, and any other necessary papers. The secretary must provide race numbers for each team member. The number should be supplied with safety pins and participants should be instructed that they be worn during the entire race. Levi Strauss will provide cloth numbers to anyone organizing a Ride & Tie event. (For more information, write to the Corporate Communications Office, Levi Strauss & Company, Two Embarcadero Center, San Francisco, Calif. 94106.) The horse should be numbered on both hips with a livestock grease-marking stick. Dark colors should be used on light colored horses and light colors on dark horses.

Awards Chairman. The awards chairman should work with the secretary and is responsible for finding sponsors to help subsidize the cost of awards. Prizes and actual money amounts, of course, will vary depending on the sponsor. Awards should be available for presentation at the completion of the event.

Publicity Chairman. The publicity chariman should make and distribute posters advertising the race to local businesses. He should also advertise the race in various publications, especially those relating to runners and equestrians. A 16-mm, 23-minute film, *What Is This Madness*, can be rented from Levi Strauss & Company's Corporate Communications Office in San Francisco. This movie could be shown locally to promote interest in the race.

Food Chairman. The food chairman should work in conjunction with the base camp chairman to assure that adequate banquet arrangements are made after the race. If food is to be provided at the base camp at other times, notice should be given.

Camp Manager. The base camp manager should arrange for a base camp and should work in conjunction with the trail chairman. Usually the camp is located near the start of the race (and the finish, if it is a loop course). Other responsibilities include arranging for portable restrooms, garbage cans, water, banquet area, preliminary exam area, and office area. The base camp chairman should use signs to designate particular areas and rules regarding smoking, fires, and so on. After the race, appropriate cleanup of the grounds should be done.

Head Veterinarian. One of the most important members of the committee is the head veterinarian. This individual must be experienced in the sport of endurance riding. A veterinarian who is not familiar with Ride & Tie will not be able to adequately safeguard against tragic consequences. It is the duty of the head veterinarian to arrange for veterinarians and arrange a "flowchart" so that each checkpoint will have enough veterinarians working to avoid horses having to wait too long to be inspected.

The head veterinarian will work with the trail chairman in determining the appropriate positions for Vet Checks and will also assure that proper emergency equipment is transported appropriately. He will assure that each veterinarian is familiar with all of the indications of stress and publish specific recovery criteria. These criteria and Vet Check instructions should be discussed thoroughly at a briefing meeting with all competitors prior to the race. A sample instruction sheet is included in Appendix II, located at the back of this book. The instructions were prepared by Dr. James Steere.

Trail Chairman. The trail chairman is in charge of finding a suitable trail. A Ride & Tie course should be challenging enough to keep the game "defensive." That is, stamina, skill, and strategy—the "three S's of Ride & Tie"—should remain the important variables, not high-speed racing. On the other hand, the trail should not be dangerous. To make sure it is not too demanding, it must be ridden in toto before a definite decision is made. If segments are marked and tested separately, a hill that was acceptable by itself could become foolhardy when combined with the rest of the course. Care should be taken to assure that all parts of the trail will be able to accommodate a large number of horses and runners without being destroyed. A bridge or a muddy creek crossing, for example, could eventually become impassable after a great deal of traffic. It is important that the trail be preridden to determine approximate minimum and maximum completion times. With the use of trail bikes, the exact mileage should be determined so that competitors will be able to pace themselves accurately. Once the trail is measured, cleared, and timed, a map should be made, with a course description attached. These maps should be sent to prospective participants and can be used for prerides. The day before the race, the trail should be marked with lime. Ribbons can be used in conjunction with the lime, but are not as reliable as lime, if used alone.

In the Levi's National Ride & Tie, helicopters are available for emergency purposes. As this is not likely in local events, the trails should be accessible by vehicle to some extent. In order to minimize other transportation problems, the course should be made in a figure-eight pattern or a circular path. This will help assure that management staff and veterinarians will be able to reach the various checkpoints in time. Although "spot-check" areas need not be accessible to pit crews, the major Vet Checks should be. In choosing the location of checkpoints, the trail chairman should be sure to consider water sources.

The trail chairman must also hire or appoint several safety riders to ride over segments of the trail to pick up or report on any injuries or problems. They should know the trail and have experience in first aid. Their horses should be in good condition and they should carry water, first-aid kits, maps, wire cutters, and rope. Arrangements should be made to have personnel posted at intersections or road crossings to conduct traffic.

Personnel Manager. A ride personnel manager is necessary to coordinate the logistics and equipment for timing and records. Responsible individuals should be hired or appointed by this official to handle the appropriate forms for Vet Checks, the number of mandatory ties made, eliminations, time in and out of each checkpoint, and finish times. The ride personnel manager should also make arrangements for a starting procedure. The traditional Ride & Tie start employs the "stampede start," which requires a large field located near the base camp. A loud speaker system is usually used for the countdown and a flag or gun is used to signal the start.

Farrier. One final position necessary is the availability of a farrier. Participants will use a farrier at their own expense, but one should be available to remedy loose or lost shoes and to reshoe those horses that must be reshod by veterinarian's orders for qualification to start or continue.

12
Conclusion

A child, a puppy,
Or a foal in the field
Know more of life and of love
Than do we.
They play without purpose,
But each moment's intense.
And until purpose comes
They stay free.

Perhaps "Cowman" Ken Shirk summed it up best when he said, "If you do it, you can't lose." This is the philosophy behind the "revolution of play" that George Sheehan describes. Through games and sports we are able to experience the true meaning of life without the distortion of interpretation, bias, fear, or insecurity. We can demand self-actualization and mutual dependency without the threat of fatality.

Ride & Tie is not a social panacea. It does, however, incorporate the concepts that may be necessary for social survival and individual happiness. Mike Spino has spoken of a "creative orientation toward integrating sport into the experience of life." Ride & Tie is such an orientation. As a sport, it has not yet been compromised to "fit in." It remains a total experience, exemplifying life's many colors. It brings back our ability to focus our entire being into one moment. It is a lifetime rolled into a day. But the sport of Ride & Tie is only an excuse. It is an opportunity for us to draw ourselves out of the muck of stagnation and aim toward our potential. It reminds us that it is effort, not talent or strength, that is important. Ride & Tie is an excuse to direct this effort toward our positive potential. It is an excuse to relearn that our bodies and minds are inseparable and that civilization should not be allowed to separate us from nature, or from ourselves. More importantly, it is an opportunity for a meaningful experience without purpose.

191

For those who want to play the game, this text was designed to provide the knowledge to do so. But for every individual who is motivated to experience a Ride & Tie event, I hope there will be a dozen who will be motivated to experience the Ride & Tie philosophy. Enjoy the experience of living, maximize your positive potential, be courageous when fate is difficult or unkind, be steadfast in your aim, have concern for those around you, and revel in the camaraderie of your teammates and competitors.

Appendix I

Exercise can be described both in terms of movement and oxygen requirement. Movement can be subdivided into *isometric* and *isotonic* exercises. Oxygen requirement includes *aerobic* exercises and *anaerobic* exercises.

Isometric exercises are muscular contractions that are static, as when pushing against an immovable object. These can be used to develop strength for an activity that requires a steady, concentrated effort. Isotonic exercises are those that involve muscular contractions that put the muscle through its full range of motion. These exercises develop strength and endurance in such activities as calisthenics, weight lifting, participation sports, and everyday activity.

The amount of effort exerted during exercises, whether isometric or isotonic, determines whether the exercise is aerobic or anaerobic. Anaerobic exercise is done at such an intensity that the muscles use up more oxygen than can be furnished to the body from the atmosphere via the heart and lungs. Such an activity can only be performed until the oxygen already present in the muscle is depleted. Anaerobic activity occurs when maximum effort activities, such as sprinting, are performed.

Aerobic exercise is performed within the body's capacity to use oxygen; i.e. the heart and lungs are able to furnish the oxygen needed by the muscle. Thus, aerobic exercise can be done for a much longer time than anaerobic exercise. Through regular aerobic training, the amount of oxygen your lungs and heart can extract from the atmosphere and furnish to the muscles increases. With an increase in aerobic capacity, you are able to perform greater work loads with less effort and for a longer duration. Such work loads may have previously required you to work anaerobically.

Aerobic capacity can be improved with the training techniques recommended in this book. Through the use of such techniques the heart muscle can be strengthened so that it can pump more oxygenated blood with fewer beats. The following tables will help you determine your present level of fitness, show you how to increase your aerobic capacity and endurance, and give you guidelines for injury-free running.

To determine your aerobic capacity, find your body weight at the top of table 1 in column A. Now find the post-exercise fifteen-second pulse count in column B. The figure in section C that forms the perpendicular coordinates of A and B is your "Aerobic Fitness Score," and should be located again in column D in table 2. In this table, locate your age in column F and connect the perpendicular coordinates of D and F in section E. This will give you your "Age-Adjusted Aerobic Score."* Your SILK rating can be determined by interpolating this score into table 3 ("Aerobic Rating") and adding the points to those totaled on the "Strength and Flexibility Rating" chart included in chapter 3. The SILK rating (in table 4) will determine the approximate number of injury-free miles you can cover in weekly Ride & Tie training.

Aerobic capacity can be measured with the "step test." This test requires that you step up and down onto a box, chair, or platform measuring 15¾ inches from the floor. This test can be used for life-long fitness measurements as well as for prerequisite Ride & Tie standards. The test has been designed to incorporate built-in penalties for weight and age. The older and heavier you are, the better conditioned you must be in order to achieve the same score as someone who is younger and lighter. This is based on the assumption that the older, heavier individual will be more susceptible to overexertion for a specific work load than a younger, lighter person in an otherwise equal condition.

The test will be more accurate if you have not eaten, exercised, or consumed coffee or tea within an hour of commenc-

---

* This score will be a projected maximum oxygen uptake in milliliters of oxygen per kilogram of body weight per minute. It should be noted that the average untrained male in the United States has an oxygen uptake of 40 ml./kg./min. compared to a champion distance runner who has about 85 ml./kg./min.

ing. The test consists of stepping up and down on the bench at a rate of ninety beats a minute for exactly five minutes. In order to time the ninety beats, you can use a metronome, a tape recorder, or simply watch the second hand on a clock as you perform. You will make one action for each beat, for a total of four actions to complete one evolution. In other words, you will be stepping up on the bench forty-five times a minute, which is equal to ninety actions per minute. If at any time during the step test your heart rate exceeds your upper limit, stop the test and retake after a week of conditioning. After exactly five minutes, stop and sit for exactly fifteen seconds and locate your pulse. During the fifteen seconds immediately following the fifteen-second rest, count your heart beats for fifteen seconds.

TABLE 1
CALCULATING AEROBIC FITNESS

Pulse count
(15 sec.) Body Weight (pounds)

A	120	130	140	150	160	170	180	190	200	210	220	230	240
B					C								
45	33	33	33	33	33	32	32	32	32	32	32	32	32
44	34	34	34	34	33	33	33	33	33	33	33	33	33
43	35	35	35	34	34	34	34	34	34	34	34	34	34
42	36	35	35	35	35	35	35	35	35	35	35	34	34
41	36	36	36	36	36	36	36	36	36	36	36	35	35
40	37	37	37	37	37	37	37	37	36	36	36	36	36
39	38	38	38	38	38	38	38	38	38	38	38	37	37
38	39	39	39	39	39	39	39	39	39	39	39	38	38
37	41	40	40	40	40	40	40	40	40	40	40	39	39
36	42	42	41	41	41	41	41	41	41	41	41	40	40
35	43	43	42	42	42	42	42	42	42	42	42	42	41
34	44	44	43	43	43	43	43	43	43	43	43	43	43
33	46	45	45	45	45	45	44	44	44	44	44	44	44
32	47	47	46	46	46	46	46	46	46	46	46	46	46
31	48	48	48	47	47	47	47	47	47	47	47	47	47
30	50	49	49	49	48	49	48	48	48	48	48	48	48
29	52	51	51	51	50	50	50	50	50	50	50	50	50
28	53	53	53	53	52	52	52	52	52	52	51	51	51
27	55	55	55	54	54	54	54	54	54	53	53	53	52
26	57	57	56	56	56	56	56	56	56	55	55	54	54
25	59	59	58	58	58	58	58	58	58	56	56	55	55
24	62	61	61	61	61	60	60	59	59	58	58	57	
23	65	64	64	64	64	63	62	61	61	60	59		
22	67	67	66	66	66	65	64	63	63	61			
21	70	70	69	69	69	67	66	65	64				
20	73	73	72	72	72	70	68	67					

To determine your aerobic capacity, find your body weight at the top of column A. Then find the post-exercise fifteen-second pulse count in column B. The figure in section C that forms the perpendicular coordinates of A and B is your "Aerobic Fitness Score," and should be located again in column D of table 2. In table 2, locate your age in column F and connect the perpendicular coordinates of D and F in section E. This gives you your "Age-Adjusted Aerobic Score."

TABLE 2
AGE-ADJUSTED AEROBIC SCORE

D Fitness Score	F Age 15	20	25	30	35	E 40	45	50	55	60	65
30	33	32	30	29	28	26	25	24	23	22	21
31	34	33	31	30	28	27	26	25	24	22	22
32	35	34	32	31	29	28	27	26	25	23	22
33	36	35	33	32	30	29	28	26	25	24	23
34	37	36	34	33	31	30	29	27	26	25	24
35	38	37	35	34	32	31	29	28	27	25	24
36	40	38	36	35	33	32	30	29	28	26	25
37	41	39	37	36	34	33	31	30	28	27	26
38	42	40	38	37	35	33	32	30	29	28	27
39	43	41	39	38	36	34	33	31	30	28	27
40	44	42	40	38	37	35	34	32	31	29	28
41	45	43	41	39	38	36	34	33	32	30	29
42	46	44	42	40	39	37	35	34	32	31	29
43	47	45	43	41	39	38	36	34	33	31	30
44	48	46	44	42	40	39	37	35	34	32	31
45	49	47	45	43	41	40	38	36	35	33	32
46	51	48	46	44	42	40	39	37	35	34	32
47	52	49	47	45	43	41	39	38	36	34	33
48	53	50	48	46	44	42	40	38	37	35	34
49	54	51	49	47	45	43	41	39	38	36	34
50	55	52	50	48	46	44	42	40	38	36	35
51	56	54	51	49	47	45	43	41	39	37	36
52	57	55	52	50	48	46	44	42	40	38	36
53	58	56	53	51	49	47	45	42	41	39	37
54	59	57	54	52	50	48	45	43	42	39	38
55	60	58	55	53	51	48	46	44	42	40	38
56	62	59	56	54	52	49	47	45	43	41	39
57	63	60	57	55	52	50	48	46	44	42	40
58	64	61	58	56	53	51	49	46	45	42	41
59	65	62	59	57	54	52	50	47	45	43	41
60	66	63	60	58	55	53	50	48	46	44	42
61	67	64	61	59	56	54	51	49	47	44	43
62	68	65	62	60	57	55	52	50	48	45	43
63	69	66	63	60	58	55	53	50	48	46	44
64	70	67	64	61	59	56	54	51	49	47	45
65	71	68	65	62	60	57	55	52	50	47	46
66	73	69	66	63	61	58	55	53	51	48	46
67	74	70	67	64	62	59	56	54	52	49	47
68	75	71	68	65	63	60	57	54	52	50	48
69	76	72	69	66	64	61	58	55	53	50	48
70	77	73	70	67	64	62	59	56	54	51	49
71	78	74	71	68	65	62	60	57	55	52	50
72	79	76	72	69	66	63	61	58	55	53	50

TABLE 3
AEROBIC RATING

If your "Age-Adjusted Score" is less than 45, your aerobic points are 0.

If your "Age-Adjusted Score" is 45 to 51, your aerobic points are 4.

If your "Age-Adjusted Score" is 52 to 59, your aerobic points are 8.

If your "Age-Adjusted Score" is 60 or more, your aerobic points are 12.

TABLE 4
SILK CHART

Number of aerobic points obtained (4, 8, or 12)
Number of strength and flexibility points obtained (0-24)
Total number of SILK points (0-36)

If your total number of SILK points are less than 11, continue doing strength and flexibility exercises in addition to an exercise other than running. Do not start weekly running mileage until your SILK points are 11 points or more.

Total SILK points	Miles to run
11 to 14	6
15 to 17	10
18 to 21	14
22 to 26	21
27 to 30	35
31 to 35	56
36	70

Appendix II

This section is designed to help those who plan to organize a Ride & Tie. It contains Dr. James Steere's "Instructions to Contestants on Vet Checkpoints and Care of Horses," a sample map of a Ride & Tie course, and a written description of the map. This written map description should be included with a packet containing rules, maps, and instructions issued to each contestant at the sign-up area.*

Instructions to Contestants on Vet Checkpoints and Care of Horses

Preride Veterinary Examination. Today your horse will get a very thorough examination. If the vet feels that your horse has any problem with his way of going, his soundness, or his condition, he will talk to you about this and tell you what you should watch for during the ride. If, from his examination, he feels there is a question about whether your horse is sound enough to go on the ride, he will send you and your horse to a second vet for examination. If, without previous consultation, the second vet concurs with the diagnosis made by the first vet, the two will then consult about the condition of the horse and make a decision as to whether the horse should be passed. If you wish to appeal their decision you may come to me. However, all the vets on this ride are experienced in three important areas:

a. equine practice
b. endurance riders in their own right
c. endurance ride judging

So, you will have to present a fantastic case for me to override the decision of any two of these vets.

*The material contained in Appendix II is reprinted with permission from Dr. James Steere, Levi Strauss & Company, and the California Horsemen's Association.

Before you bring your horse in for the examination, be sure to take him out for a little ride, warm him up, and get any stiffness or minor lameness worked out of him. Often the horse will be a little stiff or lame from a long trailer ride or may have a slight, chronic lameness that may work out when warmed up. At the same time, if you're aware of some minor problem that your horse may have, consult with the vet during the preride examination so that he can help you cope with the problem should it arise during the course of the ride.

Five Veterinary Checkpoints. These, if the weather permits, will be what we call spot checks. That is, you will come to the checkpoint and if your horse's pulse and respiration are seventy-two per minute or below, and your horse is sound and demonstrates his energy to continue, you'll be allowed out of the checkpoint immediately. It will be helpful to you and for the vet crew looking at the horse if you're able to take your own horse's pulse and respiration and avoid presenting him until he or she is ready for examination. This makes the flow of horses through the checkpoints faster, which is an advantage to you as a contestant as well as to the vets who must examine the animals. If we determine that your horse is not ready to go you'll be held for a ten-minute reexamination. If he fails to pass the ten-minute exam he will be brought back in twenty minutes; if he fails to pass the twenty-minute exam, he'll be brought back in thirty minutes; if he fails to pass the thirty-minute exam, you and the horse will be disqualified.

Postride Examination. There will be no immediate examination of the horse when you finish the ride unless there is some medical problem that needs attention. You may immediately begin to take care of your horse to cool him off and make him comfortable. Then, after one hour, you must bring your horse back for the postride examination. In making this examination our philosophy will be that, taking into consideration the stress to which the horse has been subjected over this thirty-mile ride, he must still show enough energy reserve and reasonable soundness to proceed for a few more miles if asked to do so. The pulse and respiration should be down to 72/72. Most of them by this time will be normal. All horses must pass this examination to qualify you for the completion award.

Top Condition Award. Immediately after the last team has completed the race (six hours maximum time for award qualification) all of the teams whose horses finished in one-half hour or less after the arrival time of the winning team will present their horses once again to the vets for examination. Our decision for the best conditioned award will be based on what we have found at each vet checkpoint along the way, plus the findings of the postride vet examination.

If you have no experience taking pulse and respiration:

a. Obtain a stethescope and the help of your veterinarian or some knowledgeable horseman to show you how to take pulse and respiration.

b. There will be a short seminar held several days before the race to instruct you.

Weather. If it is a very hot day and I find the horses in difficulty coming through the spot checks, I will reserve the right to make any or all the vet checkpoints a mandatory rest period of anywhere from 10 minutes to an hour. I doubt that this will be necessary, but I simply wish to mention it. If this should occur, you will all be under the same disadvantage and it will simply require you to change your strategy so that the runner does not get ahead of the horse and rider.

Horses in Stress. Two good runners can utterly fatigue all but the best conditioned horse in a race of this kind. There are two conditions that cause real trouble for the horse on the trail. The first is a severe lameness. The second is what we refer to as the exhaustion syndrome. You can feel both as you ride. With the severely lame horse you can feel that he is not going squarely under you. The exhausted horse just feels like he is running out of gas. Exhaustion may show different symptoms but it has four basic causes any one or all of which may be in operation:

a. shortage of oxygen

b. shortage of muscle glucose required for energy burn

c. too much accumulated garbage because the horse is unable to eliminate it faster than it is piling up (think of it as internal pollution)

d. inability to eliminate body heat faster than it is building up from the energy burns

The Severely Lame Horse. Stop where you are, get off your horse, check his shoes, and check for any rocks that may have wedged in. Lead your horse at a slow walk toward the nearest marshall. If your horse warms out of the lameness you may proceed. If the horse is still very lame when you come to the next trail marshall, take yourself out of the race and the marshall will signal in for help. If your horse doesn't want to move at all, leave your horse where he is and send word with the next person who passes you. If you are the last person on the trail send word with the drag-riders and they will get help to you.

The Exhausted Horse. Stop your horse. Check pulse and respiration; wait fifteen minutes; recheck pulse and respiration for 72/72 recovery and, if your horse has made this recovery and shows the desire to go on, you may proceed. If your horse is still showing lack of energy and has no desire to proceed, wait until he has enough gas in him and lead him slowly to the nearest marshall.

It is imperative for the health and safety of your animal, if he is in trouble, that we bring medical help to the horse and not the horse to medical help. Imprint this simple but important rule in your head. We have vet checkpoints every five or six miles with vets who have drugs to treat almost any problem that may come up, and finally a helicopter, which can provide help anywhere along the trail.

Water. Loss of water, or dehydration, is a serious problem on any long-distance ride, especially if it is a hot day. There is plenty of water along the way and my advice is that you should never leave the water hole until your horse has had all he needs to drink. At the same time, you can help bring down your horse's internal body temperature by using water on the skin of the horse while he is tanking up with water on the inside. Carry a plastic bag and a sponge, but do not put the sponge in the water trough. Bag the water out; put the sponge in the bag of water; then sponge your horse. Dipping dirty sponges into drinking water is forbidden.

Drugging. Although specific drug control laws vary from state to state, we will adhere to the rule of previous Ride & Tie races, which forbid the use of any drug to alleviate pain or to hype the horse within seventy-two hours before the ride without permission of the ride veterinarians.

Finally, the entire vet staff has two basic philosophies for this or any other ride:

a. to protect the health and safety of the horse

b. to let the horse proceed at the fastest pace commensurate with its ability

All of the vets on this ride admit their fallibility and it might sometime occur that we pull a horse from competition that might have been capable of completing the course. Should you become the victim of such a mistake, real or imagined, please forgive us and try to realize that the mistake was made in favor of the horse. His health and safety are more important than completing the ride.

'77 Ride & Tie Trail

Total Distance 38.95 miles

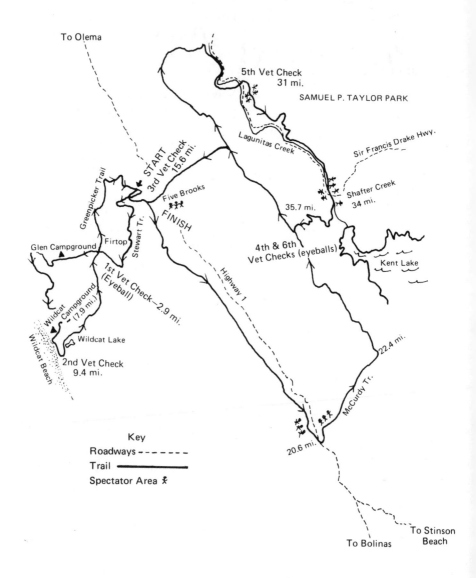

Course Description

Loop #1

Starting point for preride: Five Brooks Stable trailhead

1. Bolema trail: 5 miles south down Olema Valley. Cross Hwy. 1 at Dog Town. There will be a "trot by" Vet Check at crossing.
2. McCurdy trail: 1.8 miles 1,600 foot climb to top of Bolinas Ridge. Turn left on California State Riding & Hiking trail. There will be an eyeball Vet Check as you pass by.
3. Bolinas Ridge trail: Approximately 7.7 miles northwest down Bolinas Ridge to old N.W. railroad trail in Samuel P. Taylor State Park.
4. Old Railroad trail: Goes northeast on south side of Paper Mill Creek. One mile to Park headquarters. (This will be site of a P/R 72/72 Vet Check in the meadow by horse corrals.) Cross creek at trail by horse corrals. Cross Sir Francis Drake Blvd. and up road toward Devil's Gulch Campground.
5. California State Riding & Hiking trail: Take first trail to the right as you go up Devil's Gulch Road. Follow trail southeast which parallels Sir Francis Drake Blvd. and stops on north side of Paper Mill Creek. Trail goes 3 miles through Taylor Park, crosses creek under Shafter Bridge and goes up on the right side of creek.
6. Climb to top of Bolinas Ridge 1.7 miles. Turn right, where there will be an eyeball Vet Check and retrace trail down ridge 1 mile. Turn left down trail to Five Brooks. You can spot this turn by four signs:
   a. Hiking sign by left of road.
   b. Cattle duster on left side of trail.
   c. Stock water tank off left side of trail.
   d. You can see Five Brooks Stable below you.
7. Trail off Bolinas Ridge to Five Brooks: 1.5 miles. Halfway down ridge is a small ranch. Go to left between barn and house to avoid cattle guard. Proceed down ridge to Hwy. 1. There is a gate beside the cattle guard where road comes down to Hwy. 1. Cross Hwy. 1 and go up to Five Brooks. There will be a P/R 72/72 Vet Check there.

Total distance: 22.7 miles; total climb: 2,940 feet.

Loop #2

1. Follow Stewart trail: 7 miles up Inverness Ridge (northwest from Five Brooks).
2. Right on Green Picker trail: 1.4 miles to Fir Top. Right at Fir Top down road approximately $\frac{1}{2}$ mile where road levels out. Watch for trail to right. After you make the right turn, you will see Glen Camp sign to left.

3. Glen Camp trail: Approximately 1 mile. At first road turn left. Go approximately $\frac{1}{4}$ to $\frac{1}{2}$ mile and turn sharply back to right at first road (sign will say Coast Trail). Proceed approximately $\frac{1}{2}$ mile. Turn left at Coast Trail sign and follow trail to left and down hill to Wild Cat Beach. There will be a P/R 72/72 Vet Check here.

4. Wild Cat Beach: $1\frac{1}{2}$ miles southeast. Look for trail up cliff. At top of cliff, turn right on coast trail, approximately $\frac{1}{2}$ mile, take first road sharply back to left. Approximately $\frac{1}{2}$ mile, take first road to right (called Out road).

5. Out road up Inverness Ridge to top. Approximately ¼-½ mile, watch for trail to right. (This trail turns off approximately 50-100 feet before you get to the trail turn off you followed to Glen Camp).

6. Follow old logging road to Inverness Ridge Road. Turn left on Inverness Ridge Road, 100 yards. Turn right on Stewart trail road and back to Five Brooks—3 miles. There will be an eyeball Vet Check two miles from the finish.

Total distance: 13 miles; total climb: 2,600 feet.

Total Ride approximately 36 miles, total ride climb 5,540 feet.

Bibliography

Anderson, Bob. *Stretching.* Clark, Colo.: Bob and Jean Anderson, 1975.

Bailey, Covert. *Fit or Fat.* San Francisco: Covert Baily Press, 1976.

Beck, William S. *Modern Science and the Nature of Life.* New York: Doubleday and Company, 1961.

Costill, David. *What Research Tells the Coach about Distance Running.* Washington: American Alliance for Health, Physical Education and Recreation, 1968.

Glasser, William. *Positive Addiction.* Scranton, Penn.: Harper & Row, 1968.

Hlavac, Harry, M.D. *The Foot Book: Advice for Athletes.* Mountain View, Calif.: World Publications, 1977.

Hyland, Ann. *Endurance Riding.* Philadelphia: Lippincott, 1976.

Leonard, Jon, H.; Hofer, Jack L.; and Pritikin, Nathan. *Live Longer Now: The First One Hundred Years of Your Life.* New York: Grosset & Dunlap, 1974.

Levine, Faye. "Dangerous Encounters." *Society,* October 1973.

Rand, Ayn. *The Virtue of Selfishness.* New York: New American Library, 1965.

Spino, Mike. *Beyond Jogging.* Millbrae, Calif.: Celestial Arts, 1976.

Stevenson, Michael, and Ash, Joan. *Health: A Multimedia Source Guide.* New York: R. R. Bowker, 1976.

Toffler, Alvin. *Future Shock.* New York: Random House, 1970.

Toynbee, Arnold Joseph. *Change and Habit: The Challenge of Our Time.* New York: R.R. Bowker, 1976.

Travis, John, M.D. *The Wellness Resource Book.* Mill Valley, Calif.: John Travis Publications, 1976.

The runner's bare essentials*

Your shoes, your shorts, *Runner's World* and off you go into the world of running.

Runner's World the nation's leading running publication, has been covering the jogging/running scene since 1966. Articles for the beginning jogger through the competitive racer appear monthly. Every issue of ***Runner's World*** is loaded with good practical advice on medical problems, technical tips, equipment reviews, interviews with leading coaches & runners, and much more.

Come run with friends. Each month 510,000 fellow enthusiasts are sharing the information in the pages of ***Runner's World*** The joy of running is explored and expanded with each information packed issue—it's your coach and trainer making a monthly visit.

Exciting articles monthly: Fun Running, Run Better on Less Mileage, The Basics of Jogging, First Aid for the Injured, Running and Mental Health, Beginning Racing. Monthly columns by Dr. George Sheehan on medical advice, Dr. Joan Ullyot on women's running, Arthur Lydiard on training and racing.

Subscribe now for trouble-free miles of running. Just send $9.50 for 12 months or call (415) 965-3240 and charge to Master Charge or BankAmericard/Visa.

*Possibly because of climatic conditions or modesty you might want to add a shirt.

Runner's World Box 2680, Dept. 5534, Boulder, CO 80322